8-SECOND PR

Energize Your Story
For
Ultimate Media Success!

D0861136

Liz H. Kelly

8-Second PR: Energize Your Story for Ultimate Media Success!

© Liz H Kelly 2019

Published by *Goody PR Press*

Goody PR
(part of *Sunrise Road Media Inc.*)
Santa Monica, CA 90403
http://goodypr.com
http://8secondpr.com

ISBN: 978-0-578-42321-0

DEDICATION

8-Second PR is dedicated to the members of the Free Press who consistently focus their energy on reporting the truth and magnifying good.

And to everyone with a story to share that is making a positive impact. Stories can change the world, and we are grateful to people making a difference!

And last, this book is dedicated to my mother, Anne Heuisler, who taught English for thirty years (including having me as a student). She gave me writing genes, encouraged creative storytelling that started with home movies and puppet shows at an early age, and has been a role model for thousands of students for decades.

CHARITY

A portion of all book profits will be donated to the *Autism Society of America* to help the 1 in 59 children on the autism spectrum, adults with autism and their loved ones.

Journalism is the first rough draft of history.
—PHILIP L. GRAHAM, PRESIDENT AND CEO OF *THE WASHINGTON POST*

Table of Contents

Foreword

Foreword by Jess Todtfeld, CSP
Former TV Producer at *ABC*, *NBC*, and *FOX*
Media Trainer, Speaker, and Guinness Record-Setter for Publicity

You have in your hands a blueprint or framework to follow so you can get the attention you desire.

I know a thing or two about publicity. As a TV producer, I helped people share their messages with millions. As a media trainer and business owner, I found myself on the other side of the equation, seeking publicity to help promote my knowledge and services.

In promotion of one of my books on communication, friends in the public relations field jokingly suggested that I should run my campaign bigger than anyone else. What did that mean? Guinness record big. I accomplished it using the tactics you will learn in this book.

As I embarked on that PR journey, I looked back at my time as a producer, a "gate-keeper" to see what I had learned. As Liz Kelly will state here in this book, with eight-second attention spans, it is important for us to get our message (or pitches in this case) through—succinctly, quickly, and without any confusion. It takes years to figure out what works. After reading this book, you will learn how to work through this process, faster, easier, and with more results.

Marketing is about taking your message to the market. Publicity is powerful marketing as you are being presented to the masses by a third party. Publicity brings with it a third-party endorsement of you and what you are sharing with your audience. This endorsement is something you can use as promotion for years to come. This is one more reason why it is so valuable.

Some of the biggest secrets to breaking through and being successful in your media outreach are in the chapters of this book. You will quickly and easily learn how to grow your own PR superpowers. Figuring out your "wow" and being able to properly tell your story are some of the top strategies for connecting and winning over media gate-keepers. Surprisingly, most people pitching the media have trouble with both.

When I was on the receiving end of pitches, I booked and produced over 6,000 segments. In those 13 years, I can only imagine how many pitches were thrown out or deleted because they were confusing, did not match my outlet, or just could not communicate (quickly) why this was a story worth sharing.

Here is the good news. The media needs your help. They need it badly. And they really do want to hear from you. Why? Because they have an insatiable need for more content. That is where you come in. If you can stand out from the crowd and share stories that need to be told, many will give you the green light.

Follow the advice in this book. It will not only help you become better at the PR game, but become a better writer and better marketer, as well.

Preface

"Your Brand is Not what you say it is . . . But . . . what they say it is."

—RYAN T. SAUERS

After doing marketing and PR for over fifteen years for corporations and small businesses and booking 500+ media stories (print, radio, television and syndicated) for my best-selling dating book, I am opening up my vault by sharing our *8-Second PR* process and secrets. My goal is to provide you with first-hand insights and examples based on booking thousands of media interviews for *Goody PR* clients, along with teaching digital marketing as a *UCLA Extension* Instructor.

Because the average attention span of an adult is eight seconds, *8-Second PR* will offer new tools and tips for getting your brand name in the headlines. What we have found to be the most common challenge for many people we meet is the ability to tell a clear, concise, and compelling story. Great storytelling is a core skill you will learn in this *8-Second PR* book. And with a lot of practice and dedication, you can have immediate and ultimate media success using our *8-Second PR* Story Energizer Process!

I first fell in love with brand storytelling by defining many corporate products and services as a training executive for years who partnered with marketing pros. The most important skill I learned early in my career was to ask questions to define a powerful story. By fine-tuning this discovery process, brand storytelling became one of my greatest strengths. This "magic" or WOW is what can move your brand forward with the same speed and force as a superhero.

■ Falling in LOVE with Brand Storytelling

While working for the first *Sprint PCS* office in the United States in the Washington D.C. area, I learned from marketing pros how to tell great brand stories. Our company was called *Sprint Spectrum*, and it was a "beta test" for *Sprint PCS* in the Baltimore-Washington area only. The best part was our team was 100 percent independent of *Sprint's* Kansas City Headquarters for the first two years, so we could be creative and innovative with marketing.

When we launched *Sprint Spectrum* in 1995, no one predicted we would sell 300 percent over forecast in the first year. As the first *GSM* (*Global System for Mobile*) network in the country, we sold the first "affordable" cell phone ($99 *Ericsson* phones were the most popular). People could not get these phones fast enough, and we were on the frontline of the brand story development.

My job was to lead the corporate training team of seven professionals plus customer service interns, who trained 1,800 new employees in 18 months how to sell and support our products and services. We sat in marketing meetings with promotional pros who previously worked for *Nike, Haagan Daz*, and *Nestle* to determine the best way to train the front line employees (retail, sales, customer service, and retailers like *Best Buy*). This is where I fell in love with the whole brand storytelling and creative process.

To keep the product story simple, we would partner across teams to develop three to eight key selling points for each launch and then create *PowerPoint* "huddle packages" to train all customer-facing employees quickly. This new product storytelling process worked! And we were hooked!

When I later moved to Santa Monica, California, and worked for tech startups in the early 2000s, I always asked the team—on day one—what are the key selling points for the product? When there were blank stares in response to this question, I would then draft a bulleted list for their review.

My turning point into marketing and PR full-time started when I found myself laid-off after 9/11. No one was hiring, so I decided to write that book I never had time to do. Drawing upon my corporate and startup experiences, I used the same discovery process to learn what it took to write a good book. I wrote about forty hours per week for nine months straight, and was laser-focused.

The result was a fun and practical how-to dating book, *Smart Man Hunting: A Fast-Track Guide to Finding Mr. Right* with multiple media hooks resulting in hundreds of interviews.

Honestly, I had no clue what I was doing writing this book, except that I knew how to package a story. Book marketing experts taught me how to make the story media-friendly with great soundbites and fun examples. This creative storytelling process all started by defining the book's table of contents and key benefits for the reader.

■ How I Learned about Publishing and PR

For my first book, I approached the brand story development and publication process the same way you would approach a job. I was so passionate about the project that I would set the alarm for 6:00 a.m. to edit. (I am not a morning person and did not have a job at the time, so this early rising was really out of character). The process included coffee meetings and conferences to ask questions about these goals:

1. How to write a great book.
2. How to self-publish a book.
3. How to get a literary agent.
4. How to get a publisher.
5. How to write a great marketing plan.
6. How to pitch the media with relevant story hooks.
7. How to write a script for an interview.
8. How to provide powerful content during interviews and get invited back.

As an estimate, I probably invested over $100,000 in mostly my time, going to workshops, hiring PR firms, hiring media coaches, hiring a website developer, hiring a graphic artist, hiring a video reel editor and more. The good news is that the publishing and PR process worked. As a result, I was fortunate to secure over 500 media hits (print, radio, tv and syndicated interviews) for three versions of the same book (more on this later). My first TV interview was on the local *ABC News WMAR* in my hometown of Baltimore, Maryland, and the media magnification process grew from there (more about this later).

To make this *8-Second PR* marketing tips book simple and powerful, I have packaged everything in a fun how-to promote your business guide with an eight-step Story Energizer Process, eight PR Superpowers, case studies, and action items in each chapter to help you energize your story for Ultimate Media Success!

The goal of this *8-Second PR* book is to empower at least 1 million people to both tell their wow story and magnify their positive impact on the world.

The reality is that the most important part of marketing anything is having a moving story that makes people cheer, cry, scream, stand up, or take action. You must immediately WOW your audience (media, followers, and influencers) to attract new fans, build a loyal following, and increase your revenues.

To move brands forward, I have become a "Word Artist" who develops stories with meaning for clients and companies. If the message does not click immediately, my team and I keep reinventing the story until it results in media hits and fan cheers. We are grateful to have now worked with some *Goody PR* clients for years, because we know how to reinvent and reposition their story over and over again. For example, one of our long-term clients has had over 700 media hits in the past four years in major media outlets that include *The Wall Street Journal, Forbes, NPR, and FOX News* among others using our process (more on this later).

Marketing and PR professionals make it all look so easy, but trust me, it is not. Based on our experience, we will compare two night-and-day telecommunications company case studies in this book. Company A (*Sprint Spectrum*) sold 300 percent over forecast while Company B (*Motorola's Iridium*) filed bankruptcy after spending $7 billion—and these results were mostly due to the brand story!

If you take away anything from this book, remember this: A brand without a "Wow Story" will go nowhere fast.

Instead of your brand being a flop, we want your fans to be willing to sleep outside all night to get your book, services, or products—a scenario we have seen at San Diego's *Comic-Con International* for the past eight years.

As a marketing foundation, getting to your WOW Story includes multiple elements. It is your personal and business brand, website, and social media. It is your book, products and services, and business cards. It is what you wear, what you say, and more that all contribute to the way your brand is perceived by the world.

With 3.03 billion active social media users as of Q3 2017 (almost half the world's seven billion population), you can no longer rely on one-way marketing. While working for *Fox Interactive Media/Myspace* in 2007 and 2008, I first learned that engaging fans in two-way conversations online was the best way to increase Word-of-Mouth (WOM) Marketing.

What you need to do is get your brand message out there and have raving fans talking about it. Relying solely on paid ads like they did during the *Mad Men* advertising agency days in New York City in the 1960s no longer works. Social Media Marketing is a much faster way to reach consumers versus posting a billboard or paying big bucks for ads.

As a published author, I learned about the power of EARNED MEDIA (where someone else vouches for your product or service) for building a brand. Some of our recent *Goody PR* client interviews have included *CNN*, *FOX News*, *CBS Health Watch*, *The Washington Post*, *The Atlantic*, *ESPN Radio*, and many local TV news stories. You always want more reporters talking positively about you and your brand versus PAID MEDIA where you pay for ad space.

Earned media is worth three times more than paid media because someone else is saying your book, product, or service are great. For example, you can pay $1,000 for a TV ad to be aired during a local news broadcast or have a TV interview that is worth $3,000 in Calculated Publicity Value during the same time on the same network. Which option sounds better to you?

Once you have that magic story defined to WOW your audience, you cannot stop there. It takes a lot of hard work, powerful media hooks, good timing, follow-up, and a lot of luck to get into headline news stories.

Are you ready to energize your story with *8-Second PR*?

You can have great media success and business results with the right tips, tools, focus and story!

Let's get started!

Liz H. Kelly

Introduction

"If I was down to the last dollar of my marketing budget, I'd spend it on PR!"

—BILL GATES

Are you struggling with how to break through the noise to get media coverage in TV, radio, and print outlets so people know your name? Do you want to learn how to book a TV interview with one email pitch? And would you like to increase your awareness, credibility, and sales by having other people recommend your brand? If you answered yes to any of these questions, you are in the right place.

Your challenge is telling a clear, concise, and compelling story that hooks the media on why your message is so important to tell now.

To fast-track your promotional journey, we are going to give you a proven *8-Second PR* Story Energizer Process and eight new PR Superpowers to help you score more earned media!

To emphasize the importance of getting your message across quickly and clearly, we chose *8-Second PR* as our book title. According to a *Microsoft* consumer study (2013), the average attention span of an adult is eight seconds. And this number has been dropping. It was 12 seconds in 2000, and will probably be five seconds by the time this book is published!

If you have a personal or business brand to promote, you can magnify your story faster using an *8-Second PR* approach. You want a WOW story that makes an emotional connection like millions feel towards superhero characters. These characters not only drive millions in box office sales, they are featured stars at *Comic-Con* conventions worldwide and have hundreds of millions of fans!

To get booked on your top media picks, we will highlight how to magnify your brand with messages that hammer home. Each of the eight chapters in this book includes a PR Superpower with action items to enhance this skill. For example, we will talk about how to use your Media Hook Superpower to connect with reporters. With these new insights, you will book more interviews on your favorite news programs, national magazines, or top radio shows.

By combining all eight PR Superpowers in this book, you will be able to reach your Ultimate Media Success and goals much faster.

And you can use the new *8-Second PR* process, tools and strategies to promote both personal and business brands. Because everyone has a personal brand that they present to the world every day, you are probably one of the people who can benefit by reading this book.

■ Who Should Read *8-Second PR?*

1. Anyone who wants to have a brand be a recognized name.
2. Anyone who wants to promote a product/service, increase credibility, and/or increase sales.
3. Anyone who wants to start a new business and get new ideas for how to define the brand story, get media exposure, and build a social media following.
4. A business leader who wants to hire a marketing/PR agency to better understand the process and potential value to the bottom line.
5. Anyone who wants better control over a brand's reputation.
6. Marketing and PR professionals who want to hear another POV (point of view).
7. College and graduate school students who are studying marketing, communications, public relations, and/or journalism.
8. Baby boomers who want a crash course on the power of digital marketing.

While the majority think they can explain their story, many put people to sleep in less than eight seconds. We cannot stress enough the importance of IMMEDIATELY CONNECTING with your audience in a powerful way so that they remember you.

Great PR is about inspiring, connecting, and moving your desired audience to take action. The more entertaining and educational your story, the more the media, fans, and influencers will want to share it.

And while "Your WHY" is paramount, it is even more important to explain "WHY does it REALLY matter to your audience?" A story pitch to a reporter or producer should never be "all about you." Instead, you should include how their audience can learn or benefit.

Your brand messages need to be so compelling that people want to take a second look at whatever you are offering. While your delivery approach may be different for each marketing element (marketing, PR, social media, events, books, promotions, seminars), the story must fit together consistently.

■ Case Study Example — No Clear Message with 14 Agencies

As an example, let's take a look at a real story scenario where a major company did not have one communications plan. When we worked on the social media strategy as a marketing consultant for a major energy company in Southern California, we discovered they had already hired fourteen other marketing agencies. During the strategy process, we uncovered that each agency was sending out a different brand message.

As a result, the marketing team hosted an all-day conference with these agencies to work on consistent messaging. The result was a complex summary chart to consolidate their story. It was a great first step towards getting everyone on the same page.

Our project ended shortly afterward because they did not want to add a fifteenth agency to the mix. We walked away with the satisfaction that our greatest gift was moving them toward one story.

You must be able to tell your brand story CONSISTENTLY in one sentence. Then, once you capture your audience's attention, you can expand on the story.

WHAT IS THE WHY FOR THIS *8-SECOND PR* BOOK?

While many PR experts hold their secrets close, my goal is to empower at least one million people and brands to magnify their good through Wow

Storytelling and media coverage. Honestly, I get a charge out of making others look good and want to share advice tips on what we do best.

You can gain insights based on our unique 360-view as a former corporate executive, entrepreneur, published author, entertainment reporter, and contributor to various publications. We know what many reporters are thinking as someone who's been a contributor to the *Huffington Post*, *The Examiner*, and *Red Carpet Report*. I have also ghostwritten columns for *Entrepreneur*, *Home Business Magazine*, *Inman News*, and more.

When I took a personality profile test designed by entrepreneur coach and author Roger Hamilton, it came back that my dominant personality trait was a "Star." Roger explained that a "Star" is like Oprah—it is someone who can look good on camera, but where they really shine is making others look good. Looking back at my career, that description made perfect sense because every company where I worked (*Sprint PCS*, *Paramount Pictures*, *Fox Interactive Media/ Myspace*, and tech startups), no matter what my title was, I made other people and brands look REALLY GOOD and successful through brand storytelling.

After publishing my first book, *Smart Man Hunting*, and getting 500+ earned media hits (print, radio, TV and syndicated stories), I decided to use my marketing skills for good full-time at the end of 2008. I was no longer promoting my dating book and wanted to help others get their message heard by the masses.

■ *Smart Man Hunting* — **Three Book Versions**

To help you see the big picture of publishing, media and story reinvention, here's the progression for our dating book. *Smart Man Hunting: A Fast-Track Guide to Finding Mr. Right* was published three times over four years. Much of its success resulted from a solid marketing strategy and catchy content that attracted both readers and media.

After hundreds of media interviews, I became really good at listening to feedback and constantly revising the story to make it even more interesting for the audience.

Each of the three book releases had a new marketing campaign based on new content. The result was a solid five years of 500+ media interviews in national and local outlets, including *CNN*, *FOX News Channel*, *Lifetime*, *USA TODAY*, *Chicago Tribune*, *BBC Radio*, and more.

Book V1 2002 — Version 1 of *Smart Man Hunting* was self-published in 2002 through *iUniverse*. I hired a graphic artist to do the book cover, and it was available to purchase on *Amazon* and *Barnes and Noble* after only nine months. The version was a start and was updated in a major way for V2 and V3.

Book V2 2003 — Because the book was publicized on national TV in the first few months (*The Other Half* with Dick Clark), *Barnes and Noble* picked it up for a special program. They chose seven titles out of 12,000 self-published books in 2003. Fortunately, they assigned an experienced editor who worked with me collaboratively. The revised book featured new artwork, new content, and a book endorsement by John Gray Ph.D. (*Men Are from Venus, Women Are from Venus*) on the front cover. Version 2 was distributed in *Barnes and Noble* stores nationwide.

Book V3 2006 — After more mega media hits in national and local media, I finally found a literary agent (through a friend, Vicki Winters, who met him on *Match.com*). Fortunately, he agreed to represent me within 24 hours of our first call. In addition, he secured a publishing deal for *Smart Man Hunting* within two weeks after sending the book out to publishers for an auction. *Kensington Books* in New York published Version 3 with a new cover, new content, and the backing of a major publishing house. This book deal also came with a royalty advance at last!

Along with having a great brand, media credibility, and household name testimonials, the book included 26 fun ABC Man Codes for the different personality types. These man codes (*Bachelor Available, Justifying Juggler*) were the book's secret sauce because it provided unique, fun and relevant content that reporters loved (more on this later).

The *Kensington Books* editor said *Smart Man Hunting* V2 was so good that it did not need any edits. However, we knew the book needed NEW CONTENT for new media hooks in order to score more interviews.

To extend the marketing for the book, I re-invented pieces of the brand story with new advice tips to gain continual press. I listened carefully to fans, reporters, and media coaches to learn what people really wanted to hear. For example, I added the "First Date Kiss Test" and "Sexy Smile Test" (both were great content for TV interviews).

Liz H. Kelly

I pitched dating story topics from the book to reporters based on holidays, current trends, headline news, and relevant technologies (new dating sites, apps and more). If you are a creative person who loves to come up with entertaining topics and ways to help others, you can have a blast developing marketing and PR stories—over and over again! (We will talk more about this process throughout the book, and in Chapter 8 with Story Reinvention Superpowers).

Most of my dating book interviews for *USA Today*, *BBC Radio*, *Lifetime* and more happened while I was working at corporate jobs. Juggling media requests with a full-time job can get a little crazy - coordinating interviews, taking time off, and applying TV makeup in the bathroom. While this sounds hard, if you are truly dedicated to your brand and mission, you will make time for media.

For the best PR results, you ALWAYS want to be ready and flexible with great content when a reporter asks for an interview. However, I do caution you that this scheduling challenge can create some surreal circumstances.

■ Our Almost Oprah Moment!

During the first week of working for a tech startup in Los Angeles, I was asked by an *Oprah* producer to confirm that I could fly to Chicago to be on the show if they needed me. This request was a dream come true for any author, so despite the career risk of asking for time off at a new job, I took the gamble.

For this potential interview, the producer asked me to find a happy couple who I helped find love and confirm that they could also fly to Chicago. To be discreet, we made all our calls in the parking lot during breaks at work. "If it happened" is the key phrase here, which added stress to this juggling act.

The *Oprah* team ended up selecting Candace Bushnell (who wrote *Sex and the City*) for the segment instead of me. While most authors would scream out loud (okay, I did this too), this competition is what anyone faces when the media calls. Millions of people with your area of expertise also want to share their stories on TV. You must find ways to stand out to get any interview. I was not even close to Candace Bushnell's level as an author. Instead of getting upset, I celebrated coming so close to an *Oprah* interview with this level of competition.

Pitching your story to reporters and getting rejected are all part of this journey. When you get a media hit (a story published), take time to do a dance. Every story (blog, local and national outlets) adds up when building momentum and a media resume. You will have much better luck with smaller outlets in the beginning anyway.

Today, authors have new marketing tools and insights to propel brands forward through digital marketing. As an expert or business owner, you have endless online marketing tools that go way beyond traditional media to reach your key demographic, fans and influencers. We will talk more about building your digital PR Superpowers and lessons learned from teaching digital marketing at *UCLA Extension* in Chapter 2.

By now you might be asking, what is *8-Second PR*? Let's take a closer look.

Here is a sneak-peek of the top eight things you will learn in this quick guide.

■ *8-Second PR* will teach you how to:

1. Develop a memorable and authentic story from the heart.
2. Get to the point immediately for an emotional reaction.
3. Use attention-grabbing phrases in the first eight seconds of an interview.
4. Attract five times more Earned Media (TV, radio, and print) with a Wow Story.
5. Speak to the right audience at the right time using the right media.
6. Be entertaining and educational when presenting your brand.
7. Explain how your brand helps improve the lives of others.
8. Consistently reinvent your pitch to consistently book earned media interviews.

8-Second PR is a Story Energizer Process to make your brand propel forward. Every chapter in this book includes a list of eight action items, relevant examples, and a PR Superpower that you can implement to make your story even bigger than it is.

In this quick guide, you are going to be taken through an eight-step process for how to develop an inspiring story, maximize digital marketing, and score more media hits for your personal or business brand. You'll walk away with a plan for your Ultimate Media Success to raise brand awareness, increase sales, and change lives.

■ *8-Second PR* Story Energizer Process

1. Define Your Wow Story to Inspire Fans and Media.
2. Dominate Your Digital Bank to Increase Word-of-Mouth Marketing.
3. Write Compelling Content with Unlimited Strength to Move Readers.
4. Write Powerful Media Hooks to Connect with Reporters.
5. Target Your Audience with Media Vision to Laser Focus.
6. Make Your Interview Take Flight to Score Mega Media.
7. Hammer Home Your Interviews to Magnify Media Results.
8. Follow-up and Reinvent Your Story to Extend Media Success.

Does this Story Energizer Process sound simple? Think again. It is really easy to say and another thing to actually deliver results. It is too easy to ramble and never really get to the point. To enhance your media messages and results, I am going to teach you how to tell a story that people want to share.

And now, can we have a DRUM ROLL, PLEASE? Are you ready for your *8-Second PR* Superpowers? Here is the magic in this book that will help you magnify your brand and reach the right audience at the right time.

■ *8-Second PR* Superpowers = Ultimate Media Success

1. WOW Storytelling Superpower
2. Digital PR Superpower
3. Unlimited Content Strength Superpower
4. Media Hook Superpower
5. Media Vision Superpower
6. Interview Flight Superpower
7. Interview Thunder Superpower
8. Story Reinvention Superpower

Together, your *8-Second PR* Superpowers will compel your story forward to Ultimate Media Success. With these new superpower skills, you can become an unstoppable "Mega Brand You" superhero.

According to *Wikipedia*, "A *superhero* is a type of heroic stock character, usually possessing supernatural or superhuman powers, who is dedicated to fighting the evil of his/her universe, protecting the public, and usually battling supervillains."

> **Your mission, if you choose to accept, is to protect, promote, and propel your brand story to new heights. And with your new *8-Second PR* Superpowers and mega media exposure, you will be able to amplify your positive impact on the world.**

All of our *Goody PR* clients have a social impact goal that is much bigger than they are. We have worked with clients primarily in the health, finance, technology, and entertainment spheres and insist that they either have a charity or a higher purpose goal. For example, a few of our clients are *Rich Dad Advisors* to Robert Kiyosaki (*Rich Dad Poor Dad*), who are focused on teaching financial education globally.

Another one of our clients, *Warriors Heart*, focuses on healing warriors (active military, veterans, and first responders) struggling with addiction and PTSD (post-traumatic stress disorder). They are a for-profit residential treatment center that has a *Warriors Heart Foundation* 501(c)(3). Anyone can donate to this foundation to help heal our protectors. This foundation helps fund costs that are not covered by insurance and, in some cases, provides full scholarships.

Start thinking about how your brand can create positive change.

Why give back? It is not just about good karma. According to *Inc. Magazine*, 85 percent of consumers have a better opinion of and prefer to work with businesses and brands that support a charity they also like.

Let's be real. No one wants to hear about you all the time. Your story will be much more meaningful if you can show how you and/or your brand help others. It must be authentic and come from the heart. If a story does not align with your core, the audience will sense it immediately and go find another similar brand to support.

Everything in this guidebook is designed to help you attract hundreds of earned media interviews! We will talk about our baseball analogy for getting media interviews published later in Chapter 7 with your Interview Flight Superpower.

To give you more ideas, you will find case study examples of what has worked and what did not fly. You can gain insights based on our experience, and what we have seen other mega brands do.

We want to make it easier for you to get your story defined, shared, and magnified—quickly.

It is your time! Let's make it happen! Are you ready to ENERGIZE Your Story?

Don't procrastinate anymore.

Let's start building your Wow now!

STEP 1

Define Your Wow Story
to Inspire Fans and Media

"Publicity is absolutely critical. A good PR story is infinitely more effective than a front-page ad."

—Richard Branson

Can you gain someone's attention in eight seconds? Honestly, how long does it take you to explain what you or your business does at a busy networking event? Can you explain your brand, book, or service with passion in one sentence?

With the average attention span of adult being only eight seconds, your job as a marketer just got 100 times harder. You must make an immediate impression and create an emotional reaction, or they will forget about you.

To kick-off this *8-Second PR* book, we are going to dig deeper into developing your Wow Story in this chapter. For marketing, PR, and social media campaigns, you need ONE clear, concise, and compelling story that gets both fans and the media excited.

Even though a Wow Story is the most important factor in your business's success, it always amazes us how many business leaders and CEOs skip this step. To help your brand succeed, here is your first, and probably most important, PR Superpower. If you can master this skill, you will be able to maximize your media exposure, brand awareness, and sales results.

Let's get started!

> **■ PR Superpower 1 - Wow Storytelling Superpower**
>
> We want you to go way beyond telling a great brand story using the **Wow Storytelling Superpower**. By mastering your message, you can inspire fans, media and influencers to make your story go viral. You want to make a lasting impression that moves the reader, reporter, or customer to share your brand story over and over again. Yes, you want to find an A-team, unique product, and powerful spokespeople, but ultimately, your media results go back to the story. If you have the determination and dedication to edit your story more than 100 times to make it truly inspiring, you will have Ultimate Media Success. You've got this with your first *8-Second PR* Superpower.

For this chapter, we will review how to build your brand story so it connects on many levels, compare case studies, and look at the details for two telecommunications companies with vastly different marketing results.

While reading this book, decide whether you want to focus more on promoting one of your personal or business brands. As you go through these steps, you can immediately start applying these action items to your brand's book, product, or service.

Let's start making magic happen by reviewing the eight action items for this chapter.

STEP 1 ACTION ITEMS — DEFINE YOUR WOW STORY TO INSPIRE FANS AND MEDIA

1. Identify three life changers that drive your personal/business brand story.
2. Pinpoint what work you/your company would do for free.
3. Define your personal brand using the power of threes.
4. Define your business brand wheel driving your story.
5. Identify three to seven Unique Selling Points your brand can offer others.
6. Define your brand mission, vision, and values.
7. Find three people positively impacted by your brand.
8. Share your story. Revise it. Share again.

PR SUPERPOWER 1 — WOW STORYTELLING SUPERPOWERS

Successful marketing is always driven by a powerful story. When I was recently with a *Goody PR* client at *FOX 11 Los Angeles*, someone in the green room asked me, "Why do you think they pick one person over another for a TV interview?" My reply was, "It's all about the story."

For this *FOX 11* interview, it was for a pre-election panel discussion with three guests on "The Issue Is" show. There are thousands of experts in Los Angeles who would have loved to be on this panel. The host Elex Michaelson chose our client Danny Zuker because he had a new and relevant political humor book, is an Executive Producer for the *ABC* hit show *Modern Family*, and is a comedian. All of these things contribute to his "personal brand story" and why he was chosen for this special edition panel.

As a business brand example, let's look at the *Goody Awards* for Social Good. When developing this brand story, we met with over 20 CEOs of startups in the Los Angeles area to get their feedback on this online/offline awards program. Our pitch deck was on an *iPad*, and it illustrated the goal to inspire people to immediately recognize people, businesses, and brands doing good via social media. The lightning finally struck while I was having dinner with a CEO friend in Beverly Hills. He looked at me and said, "You are all about entertainment. We have the *Emmys*, *GRAMMYs*, and why not the Goodys?" And that was the magic moment for defining the *Goody Awards* brand.

And then we took it a step further with this title and tag line –>
Goody Awards—Recognizing Extraordinary Social Good
(more on this brand story later.)

At their peak, the *Goody Awards* had fans tweeting nominations via Twitter from over 30 countries. This program lets people vote and nominate social impact leaders for both online and offline awards to promote good. The *Golden Goody Award* (our top Humanitarian Award) has been presented to stars and organization leaders at events to call attention to their causes. Recipients have included Ian Somerhalder (*Vampire Diaries, Ian Somerhalder Foundation*), Sir Nicholas Winton (who saved 669 children from the Holocaust), Amma "The Hugging Saint" (who raised $60 million for charity through *Embracing The World*), Anna Cummins (*5 Gyres*), John Stewart (*Green School Bali*), Jeanne Meyers (*My Hero Project*), Tanya Sandis (*Free2Luv*), Budd Friedman (*Improv Comedy Club* founder), and Matt Asner (autism advocate).

Stories also have a HUGE impact on the success or failure of movies produced by the entertainment business. It is a "business" because the primary goal is to make money. However, you are never guaranteed to make money on a film without a great script and marketing plan. How many times have you gone to a movie because of a great cast only to be disappointed by the story?

For example, here are three movie flops with bad scripts. Despite having incredible star power, these films got horrible ratings.

■ Movie Story FLOPS – Great Cast, Bad Script

The Big Wedding - 7% rating on *Rotten Tomatoes*
Cast: Robert De Niro, Katherine Heigl, Diane Keaton, Amanda Seyfried, Topher Grace, Susan Sarandon, Robin Williams, Ben Barnes

Valentine's Day - 18% rating on *Rotten Tomatoes*
Cast: Bradley Cooper, Julia Roberts, Jessica Alba, Kathy Bates, Jessica Biel, Eric Dane, Jennifer Garner, Anne Hathaway, Ashton Kutcher, Jamie Foxx, Patrick Dempsey, Taylor Swift, Taylor Lautner, Queen Latifah, George Lopez, Hector Elizondo, Shirley MacLaine, Topher Grace

Grown Ups - 7% rating on *Rotten Tomatoes*
Cast: Adam Sandler, Kevin James, Chris Rock, David Spade, Salma Hayek, Taylor Lautner, Maya Rudolph, Mario Bello, Steve Buscemi, Tim Meadows, Shaquille O'Neal, Colin Quinn, Jon Lovitz, Rob Schneider

I cannot stress enough the importance of finding your Wow Story in every marketing element. Your message should be consistent across marketing campaign tactics, which may include public relations, social media marketing, websites, blogs, videos, photographs, ads, billboards, contests, promotional events, and more. Everything should revolve around a CONSISTENT clear, concise, and compelling story.

The messages should sync between your personal and business brand to make it even more genuine. People want to work with companies and individuals who "walk the talk" for whatever they represent.

For example, we previously discussed our *Goody PR* client *Warriors Heart*. As the first and only private residential treatment program in the U.S. for "warriors only" (active military, veterans, and first responders), the WHY behind their team is what makes this program so authentic. The three founders are successful treatment providers, including two in long-term recovery. In addition, the founders include a *U.S. Army Special Forces* veteran and a former law enforcement officer (LEO). In this case, the personal brand clearly represents their business brand.

This brand story definition process may take months, or even years, to fine-tune, but your mission is to start today. Do not wait another minute. The first draft is always horrible, but you will get nowhere if you do not **JUST GET STARTED!**

Test the brand story with friends, go on a walk to think about it, revise it, test it again, show it to people in the coffee shop and ask for HONEST feedback. And then revise it again—until you get to a magic moment where you can actually see the desired emotional reaction on people's faces.

■ 3 Cs FOR WOW STORYTELLING

Clear — Your story must be clear in all your marketing communications so that the message is immediately obvious. Most media use sixth-grade vocabulary in TV, radio, and print stories in order to reach a broad audience. While watching the news, I am always puzzled by people who confuse the audience with graduate-level vocabulary. I dream about having a buzzer to hit every time someone uses a fancy word on the news. Instead, you need to go to the 30,000-foot level to tell a story clearly. As a corporate training manager, we trained hundreds of trainers how to present ideas. Our advice was always "Explain it like you would tell your grandmother or a five-year-old child." This keep-it-simple approach is your way to keep the attention of the masses.

Concise — There is a delicate balance between being clear and concise. Your best bet is to use emphasis statements and the power of threes. When TV pundits say "The top three things are . . ." or "The most important thing is . . .", they are the media pros to watch closely because they know how to keep people's attention. These pundits give you a focal point so you pay more attention. Listen to what these storytelling experts say, and practice this emphasis statement approach. You can explain the details of your story later, but keep it simple in all marketing and PR to win your audience's attention.

Compelling — No matter how clear and concise you can be, words must have meaning. Your message has to hit home and connect with your audience. It is never enough to just say "buy my new, cool, shiny object." You need to include the WHY behind it and HOW it can change lives. Having compassionate people as spokespeople who can tell stories about how their life was changed forever by your product or service is the key to going from a sleeper to a WOW!

DEFINING A NEW BRAND STORY

As a *UCLA Extension* instructor for digital marketing, my students define a new business idea and become CEO of their "new company" during the first week. This new product/service is the basis of all assignments during the 11-week class. Finding the right brand name and product in Week 1 is always the hardest part for my students.

Once they find a unique brand name, students are challenged with defining their product, key selling points, five-year budget, social media plan, team, and more in a marketing plan. Their final exam is a 10-slide executive summary pitch deck that highlights their brand with charts, images, and visuals that excite their target audience.

For anyone thinking about starting a business or promoting a book, this pitch deck format is a great first step versus writing an elaborate business plan. If people do not get your idea immediately, you need to keep revising until you find the magic.

My class used to include a marketing plan final, but I changed it to a pitch deck. The visuals in a slide presentation can tell a powerful story much faster. Similar to the media, a potential investor's time is very limited. Initially, a Venture Capitalist only wants to hear your story in five-ten minute pitch. Your success with potential investors and the media is based on your ability to get to the point quickly with a powerful story!

If you are still defining your brand, consider creating a pitch deck to fine-tune your message. This ten-slide pitch deck is modeled after *Apple* marketing guru and Garage.com founder Guy Kawasaki in his book *The Art of the Start*. Once you have documented your brand using this format, schedule meetings with people who will provide honest feedback.

■ 10 Slides in a Brand Pitch Deck*

- Problem – Describe the pain you are alleviating.
- Solution – How will you alleviate the pain?
- Monetization – How will you make money?
- Underlying Magic – Describe the three to seven unique selling points/secret sauce.
- Marketing and Sales – Sales plan, digital marketing campaigns, and more
- Competition – Describe the competitive landscape. Who else is doing this?
- Management Team – Key players and core skills on your team
- Financial Budget and Projections – Your five-year plan
- Project Timeline – Three months, one year, and five years

*Based on *The Art of the Start* by Guy Kawasaki

While working for a *Goody PR* client interested in investing in technology products to help the one in 59 children born on the autism spectrum, we met with over 25 startup CEOs before finding one with a clear, concise, and compelling story. In most cases, the pitch decks were either way too long, too complex, and/or the CEO never got to the point after a one-to-two-hour meeting. In many cases, we would look at their leadership team after an hour and say, "So your product does this . . .?" And they would blush, and say, "Oh yes, that is it."

You must be able to get to the point IMMEDIATELY with fans and the media. If you see glazed over eyes when explaining your brand, hit the reset button and revise your story.

Once you have a solid understanding of your brand, it will be much easier to energize your story like a PR Superhero. Media, awareness, and sales can skyrocket if you get this part right, which is why we are spending so much time on it.

Are you ready to get started with your action items for this chapter? Let's do this!

8 STEPS TO DEFINE YOUR WOW STORY THAT INSPIRES

Step 1.1 Define Three Life Changers that Drive Your Personal Brand Story

To help you clearly define your story, go back to your personal core and think about what is most important to you. Think about life experiences and game changers that shaped your WHY. Reporters will want to know the story behind your story, so this step is really important for your PR and business success.

And if you are a marketing professional, you should do this exercise with all of your clients. Ready? Here we go.

WHAT IS YOUR STORY BEHIND THE STORY?

The first question you need to ask is what have been your top three life-changing moments that drove you towards your mission? What really inspired you to start your company, launch a product, write a book and/or choose your career? The WHY behind your story will help define your Wow Story.

It does not matter if you are selling sneakers, running a restaurant, or managing a CPA firm, there is always a story behind the story—and that starts with you. No one in the media wants to talk solely about your company. Instead, reporters want to create an emotional connection with a person. You are guaranteed to win more media and customers by speaking from the heart about why your product/service matters.

Did you know that Steve Jobs' backstory includes being adopted, taking calligraphy classes as a college dropout, being fired as CEO of *Apple*, starting *Pixar Animation*, and later being begged to return to *Apple* as CEO? All of these experiences led him to build a mega personal and business brand that has changed millions of lives around the world. What life experiences are your brand drivers?

Here are three life-changing moments behind our boutique marketing agency. As a result of these turning points, it is easier to understand the authenticity in our *Goody PR* tag line: "Let Us Magnify Your Good" through marketing, PR, and Social Media. Each of these milestones drove our story forward.

We all have stories that have impacted our brand. What have been the aha moments that drive your WHY? Can you explain your personal story using three things? For example, these are my life-changing experiences:

1. Throw your textbook in the trash can professor.
2. Business traveler stranded during 9/11 in NYC.
3. Being a published author

These three gamechangers all led me to become an entrepreneur, author, and speaker, who started *Goody PR* and the *Goody Awards*.

What changed your life so much that it compelled you to start a business, write a book, climb Kilimanjaro for a charity, give a *TEDx Talk*, and/or do what you love most? Can you explain it in a clear, concise, and compelling way?

Life Changer 1 – Throw your textbook in the trash can professor. – While going to graduate school at *Johns Hopkins University* for a master's in management, I had a life-changing professor named Barry Whitman. The first night he told our class "throw your textbooks in the trash can." We thought Barry was joking. Then, he proceeded to tell us about how he escaped from a manhole in the Korean War. Once he got out of that manhole, he made a promise that he would never live his life the same. Barry asked us to focus the entire semester on defining how we live our lives today versus how we REALLY want to live. The biggest thing Barry taught us was to think differently and make every day count. What a gift!

As a result of Barry the Professor's class, I found the courage to get divorced, moved out of my comfort zone in Baltimore, Maryland, applied for a fellowship at *The White House*, and wrote my first book—which all contributed to my story.

Life Changer 2 – Business traveler stranded during 9/11 in NYC. – My second life-changing moment was being a business traveler stranded in New York City the week of 9/11. Many people had an aha moment that week that changed their lives forever. Our company was fortunate that we did not lose anyone that week. However, I had PTSD for a long time afterward and started my personal writing again.

When the planes hit the World Trade Center's Twin Towers, I was on a train from New York City to visit our client *Aon* on Long Island. As you can imagine, the *Aon* employees were in panic mode when we arrived. Sadly, the company lost 176 people in the towers that day. The next 24 to 48 hours included being stranded when the trains stopped, military planes flying over us, and feeling very alone when the world seemed to be ending.

During my personal healing process after the trauma, I wrote a 20-page diary about my week in NYC and tried to get it published in a newspaper. And then ironically, after saving every client contract for my employer, I was laid off.

All of this experience led me toward my destiny to become an entrepreneur and focus on making others look good! I just did not know it at the time. What pushed you forward towards your passion?

Life Changer 3 – Being a published author. – When the newspapers did not pick up my stranded business traveler story, I decided to write a book about a more uplifting topic. Everyone told me to write about something that I felt so strongly about that I would not get discouraged by naysayers. Because I had a history of giving people relationship advice as "Dr. Liz" in high school and was currently navigating the Los Angeles dating scene, I decided to write a dating book. No one was hiring, especially at the corporate executive level. This new dream project kept my spirits up. Writing a book was on my "life goals wish list" in Barry the Professor's class. There was just never enough time to write when working 60-hour weeks at corporate jobs.

Throughout this book promotion process, I realized that I did not want to be famous. I wanted to make others famous. I wanted to MAGNIFY GOOD!

With these enhanced marketing skills, I started *Goody PR* at the end of 2008. Since then, my team and I have embraced redefining stories, developed fun marketing campaigns, and gotten our clients thousands of interviews with major national and local media. This earned media transformed many of their businesses—and it all started with a Wow Story.

Because of these life experiences, *Goody PR*'s "Let Us Magnify Your Good" tag line is authentic and true to my personal and business brand.

So, what are your three life-changing events that drive your personal brand and/or motivate your company? Everyone has a story, and the keywords for these moments will help you define your Wow.

Step 1.2 Pinpoint What Work You would do for Free

To find your real authentic driver, think about what you would do for free. The WHY behind your story is what will make you and your brand successful. If your work is only about money, it will be much harder to have long-term success. Anyone can create a new brand, but to get to the Wow, you have to dig deeper into what motivates you.

When you are willing to work for free, your passion takes over as the main driver. People can tell when you are really excited to help them succeed, so this is a serious question to consider.

For example, every time I hear that my work had a positive result on a client's business and sales, I am ecstatic! Every time a client gets an interview, I am so happy for them. I cannot wait to share the story everywhere on social media.

And this "enthusiasm" was the main reason *Modern Family* executive producer Danny Zuker hired me to promote his political humor gift book, *He Started It!: My Twitter War with Trump* (September 2018). I LOVE Twitter and that Zuker donated 100% of his author profits to charity (more on this later). As a result, I was so passionate about this project that we did a lot of extra work for free (which we do often for VIP clients).

In addition to doing extra work "pro bono" for VIP clients who are on a monthly retainer contract, we did free work for almost a year to get our *Goody PR* business started. My initial "free" work has paid off 100 times over the past ten years with a great portfolio of success stories, steady referrals and long-term clients.

My first pro bono work was PR for *Rich Dad Hawaii.* This group was working with Robert Kiyosaki's *Rich Dad* team to build a franchise. The founders hosted several *CASHFLOW ® Board Game* Clubs on the island of Oahu, Hawaii, along with entrepreneurial training events. For this initial marketing and PR job, I donated all of my time for free—including paying travel and expenses to Honolulu from Los Angeles. When I secured media interviews for *Rich Dad Hawaii* on every local TV news station in Honolulu, the main *Rich Dad* team in Scottsdale, Arizona, started paying attention.

For my second "partially free" job, I did a four-month integrated marketing, PR, and social media campaign for the launch of *Rich Woman* Financial Education. The event promoted Kim Kiyosaki's new program and *Rich Woman* book. I worked with the *Rich Dad Hawaii* Project Director Lee Ann Del Carpio and her global team of entrepreneurial women. As a result, about 120 people from six countries attended this launch program. Once again, we got great media coverage from the local TV news and a feature story in *Hawaii Business Magazine.* In this case, I was reimbursed for expenses, but that was it.

Liz H. Kelly

However, this *Rich Woman* Marketing Campaign led to securing one of our most loyal and long-term clients. Author, entrepreneur, social capitalist and *Warriors Heart* Founder Lisa Lannon was on the *Rich Woman* Event Committee and saw my work. As a result of building a great PR partnership, Lisa has been a steady client for most of the past ten years.

After securing 53 TV interviews for Lisa Lannon's business, *Journey Healing Centers*, over five years, the firm was sold to the most prominent company in their residential treatment niche. The buyer (*Elements Behavioral Health*) kept the brand name that we had steadily promoted in the news. Lisa and her husband, Josh Lannon, then used the money to start *Warriors Heart*. They had seen veterans and first responders struggle when mixed with civilians in drug and alcohol addiction treatment. As a result, *Warriors Heart* was opened to heal "warriors only" struggling with chemical dependencies, PTSD and recurring issues in a safe place with peers. I will cover more about their brand and marketing success stories throughout this book.

In another case of working for "a low fee," I managed clients for a successful PR agency in Beverly Hills, California. The company had represented over 50 *Academy Award* winners and several U.S. Presidents for over 30 years. In this case, we worked for a much lower monthly fee. However, it was so worth it! We learned best practice processes and new tools that made our business much more efficient and successful.

While you cannot do everything for free, the *Rich Dad Company* recommends that you donate ten percent of your profits to charity. If you donate your time, it is actually even more valuable because time is limited and one of your greatest assets.

To give back, *Goody PR* has done one major PR campaign pro bono per year around a *Golden Goody Award* (top humanitarian award for the *Goody Awards*). This campaign recognizes social good leaders and raises awareness of their charities. In addition, *Goody PR* has managed cause-marketing campaigns for paid sponsors and clients recognizing good.

While you have to set boundaries on "free work," you should love what you do so much that you would do it all day long for no pay. I love promoting people and businesses so much that I honestly never want to retire. What would you do for free?

Step 1.3 Define Your Personal Brand using the Power of Threes

I cannot emphasize enough the power of laser-focus branding. When someone meets you at a networking event, how do you describe yourself by using only three key points? Remember, you only have eight seconds to grab their attention.

Honestly, no one wants to hear your whole life story—unless you are a rock star in your niche. Getting to your point right away builds rapport much faster. Humor, tone of voice, and body language also play a critical role in making first impressions, especially when telling your story. Think about what you might say, and practice it with enthusiasm and a smile until it gets the right response.

To give you more ideas, here are examples of how we branded some of our PR clients and personal brand. In all cases, you can also see how the personal and the business brands overlap.

■ Personal Brand Examples – What Do You Do?

Realtor to the Stars and Philanthropist Debbi DiMaggio – They call me the Realtor to the Stars because I'm Joe DiMaggio's cousin and have a lot of celebrity clients. Joe's love for Marilyn Monroe is the same passion that I have as a top one percent Realtor in Beverly Hills and the Bay Area. My role model is Lady Diana, and I have adopted five charities. People say that I am a **passionate philanthropist, connector and luxury realtor**.

Autistic Animator and Advocate Dani Bowman – I want to be the Temple Grandin of my generation as an autism advocate. As an animator with autism, I empower others on the spectrum by teaching animation and entrepreneurial skills. We want to help them learn new skills and find jobs. People say that I'm a **business-savvy entrepreneur, autistic advocate and animator**.

Think about how these personal brands define their top three qualities. How would you describe your key strengths using the power of threes?

Every person is a brand. Whether you are a celebrity, author, CEO, or citizen making a difference, you have a story. It is what people think of first when they hear your name. Think about some of the mega brands you see, like Beyoncé and Richard Branson, and how their personal and business brands are in sync.

■ Mega Personal Brand Case Study 1 — Beyoncé

As a mega brand, Beyoncé is an American singer, songwriter, actress, and businesswoman. Did you also know that she grew up in Houston with parents who supported her journey? Her mother was a hairdresser, and her father was in sales.

Beyoncé started rapping and singing in a group called *Girls Thyme* at eight years old on the Houston talent-show circuit. Her brand story gained power as she became the lead singer of *Destiny's Child* in the 1990s (her sister Solange was a backup singer in this band). Her father quit his job to help manage her career, and her brand name, Beyoncé, came from her mother's maiden name. The pressures from building Beyoncé's brand contributed to her parents' divorce. When *Destiny's Child* split up in 2006, Beyoncé released her second solo album *B'Day*, which included ten top singles such as "Irreplaceable" and "Déjà Vu." After selling 100 million records and winning 22 *GRAMMYs*, Beyoncé is now one of the most recognized global brands. (Source: *Wikipedia*).

There is a lot more to Beyoncé's personal brand story, and it did not happen overnight. Just like your personal brand, a Wow Story can take decades to develop. Beyoncé's is a mega star who is recognized worldwide as a **bold, confident, and empowering artist**.

Sir Richard Branson is another mega personal and business brand. As a business owner, investor, and philanthropist, he oversees his *Virgin Group*'s control over 400 companies.

■ Mega Personal Brand Case Study 2 – Sir Richard Branson

Did you also know that Richard Branson was the oldest of three children? His mother was a former ballet dancer and airline hostess (Eve Branson), and his father (Edward James Branson) was a barrister. As a student with dyslexia and poor grades, Richard told his teacher that he would "end up in prison or be a millionaire." Branson's first business venture occurred when he was 16 and started a magazine called *Student*. In 1970, at the age of 20, he set up a mail-order record business, which later became *Virgin Records* and *Virgin Megastores*. He bought *Virgin Atlantic Airline* in the 1980s as his business grew at warp speed.

Sir Richard Branson was knighted in 2000 for his "services to entrepreneurship." Telling the rest of his entrepreneur story could take this entire book. Branson is also a humanitarian recognized for his environmental efforts. (Source: *Wikipedia*)

Liz H. Kelly

While anyone with a mega personal brand is under a microscope, Branson has kept his positive attributes in the headlines. You can summarize Sir Richard Branson's personal brand's three qualities as a mega businessman who is an **innovative, fearless, and social entrepreneur.**

Now that we have looked at these personal brand examples and stories, let's take a closer look at business brand examples.

Step 1.4 Define Your Business Brand Wheel Driving Your Story

Your personal brand should align with your business brand. If you are following your true WHY and would work for free, you will be able to propel your business forward. Look at all the drivers on your brand wheel as potential media stories.

When someone asks you to describe your business brand, find ways to make it fun and interesting. No matter what you say, add ENERGY to your story. Speak with conviction and deliver the message with a smile. The minute you take yourself too seriously, you will lose your audience.

One of the many reasons this delivery is so important is because authors must OWN their brand story when talking to potential customers and the media. If you are not confident in your WHY, a producer will never risk having you on a radio or TV interview.

Let's take a closer look at some case study examples of the power of compelling brand storytelling.

■ Case Study Example – Personal and Business Brand Match

One of our long-term *Goody PR* clients is Tom Wheelwright, who is a CPA, CEO and Author of *Tax-Free Wealth*. As a tax and wealth expert, Tom truly LOVES taxes more than anyone you will meet! His passion is to legally save people 10-40 percent permanently on their taxes, and it comes across in every media interview. This authenticity and enthusiasm are the foundation of his personal and business brands.

Tom Wheelwright's Personal Brand — While most people run the other direction when you say taxes, Tom's personal brand message is "I make taxes fun, easy, and understandable." This message is PR gold because it is clear, concise, and compelling—and will make you look twice. It also uses the power of threes to grab your attention.

Tom Wheelwright's Business Brand — After running a CPA firm for over twenty years, Tom created a new tax and wealth strategy and education company called *WealthAbility*. The company's motto is to help you to make "Way More Money" and pay "Way Less Taxes." For this business, Tom's team consults with clients to build tax and wealth strategies; provides educational tools; and is building a national network of CPAs. In support of this brand, he hosts *The WealthAbility Show* with Tom Wheelwright CPA podcast.

When the *National Association of Realtors* called to ask Tom to be a keynote speaker at their conference, it was 100 percent because of his Wow Story. How many CPAs do you know who make taxes "fun, easy, and understandable"?

When we work with clients on their brand story, we always start with the big picture, key selling points and slides. Visuals can help you see what a story may look like much faster with pictures, graphics, and videos.

For example, I worked with the creators of the *Personalogy™* game in 2016, to better define their brand story in preparation for a product pitch to retailer buyers. For this fun and entertaining card game, *Goody PR* partnered with the founders on their one-sheet and press release that contributed to getting their product into *Walmart*!

■ Brand Story Case Study – *Personalogy*™

Business Brand

Personalogy™, the LOL personal Trivial Pursuit-esqe card game instantly gets people mingling, talking, laughing and having fun! A "Party in a Box", the perfect gift that guarantees to reduce stress. It quickly turns awkward social moments into hilarious fun, and lightens the mood.

Personal Brand - Founders

Interact Games LLC is founded on the belief great conversations = great relationships. Entrepreneurial duo, Michelle Burke, Communication Expert and Author from Los Angeles, and Lilamani de Silva, Co-creator, from London met in Seattle 15 years ago. Michelle developed *TeamBuilder*™ games and piloted it at a *Microsoft* conference, and received feedback that people wanted to play the game at home. After partnering with Lilamani, they recognized a bigger need and developed *Personalogy*™ Games for the consumer market.

Do not kid yourself into thinking this brand story process is easy—lightning will not hit overnight! You will need to have a lot of brainstorming meetings, walks, and meditations to get there.

Think about if you had to present your personal or business brand story in 30 seconds on the phone, in a meeting, or to the media. What would you say? How would you engage your audience to care?

As you read this book, take notes separately on the action items you want to take for a personal or business brand. You will also find a great summary in the Conclusion of this book with the eight-step process, eight PR Superpowers and your next step challenges.

If you work for a company, think about new ideas you want to propose to your team in your next marketing meeting. Get creative about defining what makes you unique so you can get a reporter's attention. Keep in mind, there are a lot of experts who do what you do. How are you different?

■ WHY should a reporter interview you?

In all cases, you always want to define your personal story WHY before approaching any media. When you talk to a producer or reporter, many want to know your story first before booking an interview about your book or business. People connect with stories first. You must be able to explain what makes you both unique and the best spokesperson for them to interview.

Taking a brand story to Wow can require hard work, research, and interviews to get to the core.

Let's take a closer look at a mega brand case study that frequently gets discussed in my digital marketing class. This campaign is a great example of how to take a non-emotional product and turn it into a Wow Story.

■ Case Study Example — *Dove Real Beauty Sketches*

While *Dove* is a personal care brand owned by *Unilever*, their products are very boring in a crowded and competitive market. *Dove* sells antiperspirants, body washes, beauty bars, lotions, hair care, and facial products.

To make a powerful emotional connection to their target market, they developed a BRILLIANT *Dove Real Beauty Sketches* marketing campaign that connected on many levels to millions of women.

For this campaign, women were asked to describe themselves to a sketch artist, who then drew what the individuals perceived as their own image, all while being videotaped.

The artist then asked a stranger to describe the same person. The artist did a second sketch of the individual based on the stranger's description and videotaped it.

When you compared the two sketches, the first sketch with the individual's perception was much less flattering than the second sketch based on a stranger's description.

The bottom line message to women from this campaign was You are More Beautiful Than You Think, and the videos were mega hits online!

This case study is a classic example of how you can take a really boring brand and turn it into a powerful Wow Story! This story is relatable, timely, and compelling.

To give you a closer look at the importance of defining a business brands, here is a marketing case study comparison of two companies in the wireless telecom industry where I worked early in my career. The two companies had night-and-day marketing results because of their brand stories.

BUSINESS BRAND STORYTELLING – TELECOMMUNICATIONS CASE STUDY COMPARISONS

While there are many pieces to this business-branding success story and tragedy, this comparison between the first *Sprint PCS* office in the United States and *Motorola's Iridium* Satellite company offers great learning lessons about why the brand story matters enormously. Both companies were located in the Washington D.C. area.

I was fortunate to work for the first *Sprint PCS* in Bethesda, Maryland, which was a huge marketing success that transformed lives and the wireless industry in 1995. During this job, I learned invaluable skills for product storytelling.

At the time, only rich people and sales professionals could afford cell phones. This beta office was officially called *Sprint Spectrum*, and we had record-breaking sales. In comparison, *Motorola's Iridium* satellite phone company was also based in the Washington D.C. area and was a complete financial and marketing flop. The story behind these two brands provides key insights for anyone with a product to sell.

Sprint Spectrum versus Motorola's Iridium

To get to the point, here is a big picture comparison snapshot with what happened in each case.

Marketing Element	Sprint Spectrum (first Sprint PCS in US)	Motorola's Iridium Satellite Phones
Brand Story	Clear, concise, and compelling message	Mixed messages developed by 16 regional gateway offices
Key Selling Points	5 key benefits on a wallet card given to everyone	No key selling points published
Pricing	Very affordable, $99	Way over-priced, $4,000
Overcame Objections	Yes – "First minute of incoming calls free"	No – The majority did not need a brick-size phone that did not work in a city & cost $11.00/minute.
Team	50/50 Telecom & non-telecom hires	Primarily telecom & government hires
Corporate Culture	Product-driven, fun, teamwork, gratitude, big bonuses for employees	Bureaucratic, political BS!, corporate walls between departments and levels, very unhappy people
Results	**Sold 300 percent over forecast, Sold to Kansas City HQ**	**Filed bankruptcy, sold in desperation for $25 million, lost $7 billion**

Sprint Spectrum in U.S. Triumph

How did this *Sprint Spectrum* success story happen? It was a combination of a great team, affordable product, and a Wow Story! Let's take a closer look at the drivers of this HUGE marketing win.

1. Clear and Concise Message – Our overall product message was "*Sprint Spectrum*—The all-in-one Personal Communications System that goes with you." It was a cellphone and a pager (with text messaging services post-launch), all in the palm of your hand.

2. Hired 50/50 Telecom and No Telecom Experience – One of the most brilliant things that the senior management team decided to do was hire 50 percent of employees with telecom experience and 50 percent with no telecom background. They wanted the phone marketed differently, like a retail product.

3. Defined the Key Selling Points for Every Product Launch – To make it simple and easy, we worked across departments to create "wallet cards" with the key selling points. Defining what makes your brand different is my favorite thing to do for any client. I cannot emphasize this point enough. If you cannot write the top five selling points for your product or brand, stop all marketing initiatives!

4. Created a Product-Driven Corporate Culture – More important, we helped develop a product-driven corporate culture with brand ambassadors. To get everyone walking-the-talk, every employee was required to attend product sales training plus listen to customer service calls for at least one hour on their first day during the corporate orientation. Everyone in the company was told, no matter what department you are in, you are in sales!

5. Encouraged Viral Marketing – The golden ticket was the marketing team's gift to every employee. Everyone received a free phone with 1,000 free minutes (this was when cellphone companies charged per minute). And if we called a fellow employee, the call was free. As a result, employees turned into early adopters and brand advocates. Employees would literally walk up to strangers in bars in Washington D.C. and ask, "Do you want to try a cell phone call?"

6. Took Away Objections – Because we were selling people on a new technology, we wanted to overcome their fear of running up a big bill. Because no one wanted to share their cellphone number with per-minute charges, our marketing team decided to make "the first minute of incoming calls free." This one feature changed everything. Suddenly, everyone gave out their numbers and got hooked.

This *Sprint Spectrum* product storytelling example has so many great learning lessons for marketers. The sales results were off the charts! The company's story was featured on the cover of major magazines as the fastest growing telecom company in the nation. This corporate experience was my all-time favorite job where I really saw the power of brand storytelling, marketing, and working with a passionate team. Many of us worked 60 to 70 hours a week without a complaint. Once I even shared a hotel room with five people during a blizzard to meet our deadlines. And we loved it!

Motorola's Iridium Satellite Phone Product Fail

After the *Sprint Spectrum* office was officially sold to *Sprint PCS* in Kansas City, Missouri, two years after launch, the majority of our jobs were cut. A few were asked to move to their mid-west headquarters, and most found other telecom jobs in the area. Many of us accepted jobs at *Motorola's Iridium* satellite phone company who had offices in downtown Washington D.C. and Reston, Virginia.

The only problem was that *Iridium* was a completely different corporate culture, experience, and brand story disaster. *Iridium* spent $7 billion putting 77 satellites up in the sky with little to no return on investment.

Here is why this brand story became one of the biggest marketing failures in telecommunications history:

1. Mixed Messages in Tag Line and Logo – *Iridium's* tag line and only key selling point was that you could stay in touch "Anytime, Anywhere." This promise worked most of the time, unless you were in an "urban canyon" with big city skyscrapers. Honestly, why would you buy a phone that did not always work if you lived in a city? The company also spent big bucks to develop a logo that had very little creativity and looked like the Big Dipper. This logo was immediately criticized for looking like the flag of Alaska. There was very little brand identity, and the lack of communication across departments and global offices showed.

2. No Central Marketing Message – To reach a global market, *Iridium* was set up like a big government agency with about 600 employees and consultants at the Washington D.C. headquarters. They also set up 16 gateway offices around the world. Each gateway office managed a territory and was asked to define their own marketing messages for their regional customers. This lack of a central message resulted in mass global confusion over the product.

3. Way Too Expensive and Clunky –The *Iridium* satellite phone was shaped like a brick and priced way out of the market. The retail price

was a whopping $4,000 versus the $99 *Ericsson* phone that you could buy through *Sprint Spectrum*. The $99 cellphone worked much better in cities, so why would anyone buy an *Iridium* phone?

4. Marketed to the Wrong Customer – Another HUGE mistake the senior marketing team made was focusing efforts on selling to the horizontal markets (you and me) versus the vertical markets (maritime, military, and emergency services). By the time the company figured out that the vertical markets had much bigger budgets and a need for remote communications, *Iridium* had already filed for bankruptcy.

5. Bad Brand Story – At this point, my job was operations training manager with a team of 20 employees/contractors. All of the 16 global gateway offices were trained in Customer Care, Billing, Fraud and Inventory Management. However, no one was selling phones. The marketing training team had only one person, and we started getting calls for help. My *Sprint Spectrum* colleagues, who now worked for *Iridium*, called in a panic to say, "Liz, they are making paper airplanes in sales training. We need your help." Because of the dysfunctional bureaucracy where this level did not talk to that level, it was almost impossible for me to get involved. It literally took my boss three months to persuade the marketing Vice Presidents to let my training team help.

6. When our team finally got involved, we discovered that Sales was trying to sell a technology story with no emotions. Representatives would try to close major corporate contracts based on the fact that there were 77 satellites up in the sky. They would draw pictures of the satellites and say you could call Mumbai, India, from Washington D.C. for only $11.00 per minute (no exaggeration here). And P.S., the phone is $4,000 per person!

7. Too Little, Too Late – When they walked the *Iridium* CEO out of a board meeting and the company filed for bankruptcy, it was too late. The new interim CEO from South Africa said in an all-employee meeting, "We have 120 people in marketing, and if anyone can tell me what the h*** they do, I'd like to know." The next day, he laid off half of the marketing team. Then, miracles started to happen, but it was too little, too late. We put twenty marketing members in a room and brainstormed until we came up with five key selling points and a powerful product story. With this foundation, I told my operations training team, "We need to make these boring satellite phones sound sexy." They worked long hours building the story and a two day product training program.

In the end, the new *Iridium* story became "If you are working on an oil rig in the Indian Ocean and the power goes out for days, and you have no cell service, wouldn't you like to have a satellite phone with a solar charger that can save your life?" Sales went up 40 percent in six weeks. However, it was not enough to save the company. It was always about the story, and it was mind-boggling that 120 people in marketing missed the mark.

Step 1.5 Identify three to seven Unique Selling Points Your Brand can Offer Others

Most people skip the step of identifying the three to seven unique selling points for a brand. When you think about superheroes, they all have a few superpowers that make them unique. Think about your personal and business brand's superpowers. For example, can your brand save lives, find dream homes, provide electrical power, make someone famous, help people lose weight, save millions over a lifetime and/or bring joy to your customer?

Brand superpowers matter to the media and to your customers. If you can clearly define and show how your product or service can change lives, you will get many more earned media interviews, achieve your goals, and increase sales—and that is what we are here to help you do.

Do you remember *Warriors Heart*? We consistently partner with their team to build the core messages and then continually develop new and timely media hooks to stay relevant and timely. It is easy to feel inspired by this company, and their Wow Story is the basis for all of the media pitches, press releases, and coverage.

Let's take a closer look at their tag line and key benefits and results.

■ *Warriors Heart's* Tag Line and Key Selling Points

Warriors Heart tag line is "Strength Through Healing"

Based on pitching *Warriors Heart* to the media, below are the seven key selling points (starting with verbs) that we like to highlight:

1. Offers the first and only private and accredited residential treatment program in the U.S. for "Warriors Only" (active military, veterans, and first responders).

2. Helps warriors overcome their "Warrior at Home" and reduce the unacceptable average of 20 veteran suicides per day and one Law Enforcement Officer suicide every 62.5 hours in the U.S.
3. Removes the shame or stigma many warriors feel when mixed with civilians. Other than the *VA* (*Veterans Administration*), there is no other place in the U.S. that veterans can go to heal from addiction and PTSD with "peers only".
4. Offers evidence-based approaches, holistic healing, and long-term recovery using a "whole body" approach (addiction and PTSD treated in one place).
5. Provides holistic healing by a team of licensed clinicians and professionals with warrior experience (either directly or indirectly as a family member).
6. Heals "warriors" with dignity and respect on a 543-acre ranch that does not feel like a hospital with fishing, a private chef, hiking, metal shop, martial arts and more.
7. Rebuilds lives with long-term recovery tools so warriors can go back to work and their loved ones.

When you hear the phrase, there is nowhere else you can do _____, how would you fill-in-the-blank for your brand?

Step 1.6 Define Your Brand Mission, Vision, and Values

Mission, vision, and values are also major identifiers for your Wow Story. Many underestimate the importance of this step. Most business leaders are too busy building the details rather than looking at the big picture strategy, story, and marketing plan for their business. These brand cornerstones can make or break your business, so do not pass go until you've documented this core part of your brand identity.

If you do nothing else, define your brand's mission. Let's look at examples from some of the biggest brands out there as examples.

MEGA BRAND MISSION STATEMENT EXAMPLES

Nike Mission: To bring inspiration and innovation to every athlete in the world.

Oracle Mission: We help you simplify your IT environment so that you can free up money, time, and resources to invest in innovation.

American Express Mission: Be the world's most respected service brand.

MEGA BRAND MISSION AND VALUE STATEMENT EXAMPLES

Here are examples of mega brands with a mission and vision to give you more ideas:

Amazon

Mission Statement: "We seek to be Earth's most customer-centric company for four primary customer sets: consumers, sellers, enterprises, and content creators" (2013).

Vision: "Our vision is to be Earth's most customer-centric company; to build a place where people can come to find and discover anything they might want to buy online."

Apple

Mission: "*Apple* designs Macs, the best personal computers in the world, along with OS X, iLife, iWork, and professional software. *Apple* leads the digital music revolution with its *iPods* and *iTunes* online store. *Apple* has reinvented the mobile phone with its revolutionary *iPhone* and App store, and is defining the future of mobile media and computing devices with *iPad*."

Vision: "We believe that we are on the face of the earth to make great products and that is not changing." (Tim Cook)

Walmart

Mission: "Save people money so they can live better."

Vision: "To become the worldwide leader in retailing."

Toyota

Mission: "To create a more prosperous society through automotive manufacturing."

Vision: "To achieve long-term stable growth with the environment, the global economy, the local community it serves and its stakeholders."

Verizon

Mission: "Enable businesses and people to communicate with each other."

Vision: "Advance in technology that touches people's lives."

CVS Caremark

Mission: "We provide expert care and innovative solutions in pharmacy and healthcare that are effective and easy for our customers."

Vision: "We strive to improve the quality of human life."

BMW

Mission: "The *BMW Group* is the world's leading provider of premium products and premium services for individual mobility."

Vision: "To be the most successful premium manufacturer in the business."

SMALL BUSINESS MISSION, VISION, AND VALUES EXAMPLES

In addition, here are some small business examples:

Lyft

Mission: "Our mission is to reconnect people through transportation and bring communities together."

Vision: "Ride by ride, we are changing the way our world works. We imagine a world where cities feel small again. Where transportation and tech bring people together, instead of apart. We see the future as community-driven and it starts with you."

Uber

Mission: "Make transportation as reliable as running water, everywhere, for everyone."

Airbnb

Mission: "The mission is to live in this world where one day you can feel like you are home anywhere and not in a home, but truly home, where you belong."

Goody PR

Mission: "We seek to Magnify the Good in Brands through Wow Storytelling that breaks through the noise, increases sales, and changes lives!"

Vision: "We strive to magnify the good of at least one million social impact brands and influencers through our marketing services, books, and training."

Values: Gratitude, Passion, Integrity, Innovation, Fun, and Balance

You can do this too! Start writing down ideas with your team and be a Word Artist and/or hire someone to do it for you.

Step 1.7 Find Three People Positively Impacted by Your Brand

What most people do not understand is that your brand story is ten times more powerful if it includes how you helped someone else. Whether it is curing cancer, helping people communicate faster with better technologies, saving people money, or moving them to take action with a story (movie, book), you should always be asking "why does my product or service matter to anyone?"

For example, our tax and wealth expert client, Tom Wheelwright, has transformed hundreds of thousands of lives by teaching people how to legally reduce their taxes. However, this brand story cannot always be about Tom. When the *Wall Street Journal* featured Tom's tax tips for how the new *Tax Cuts and Jobs Act of 2017* will impact many small businesses, they also wanted to highlight how one of his clients is using his advice.

In another scenario, *CBS Health Watch* wanted to do a feature story about *Warriors Heart* for *Veterans Day*. This media hit was one of our biggest success stories for a client that we will cover in detail in Chapter 8 (saving the best for last)!

Step 1.8 Share Your Story. Revise it. Share again.

Most importantly, your Wow Story must be constantly updated. As you get more feedback from your customers, clients, and the media, you will quickly learn what people really want to hear, how to explain it, and how to show the positive impacts.

Once you have your story defined, your job is to build marketing campaigns, headlines, press release titles, website, photographs, videos, and social media that move people to take a second look.

It is a constant writing and rewriting process. Eventually, you will let go and publish your brand story to the world. We will keep talking about this story reinvention process throughout this book because it's so important!

CHAPTER 1 RECAP

We hope you now have some new ideas for defining an inspiring brand story with a clear, concise, and compelling message. Are you ready to edit your story 100 times to define a brand story that inspires? You can do these action items and make it happen!

Step 1 Action Items — Define Your Wow Story to Inspire Fans and Media

1. Identify three life changers that drive your personal/business brand story.
2. Pinpoint what work you/your company would do for free.
3. Define your personal brand using the power of threes.
4. Define your business brand wheel driving your story.
5. Identify three to seven unique selling points your brand can offer others.
6. Define your brand mission, vision, and values.
7. Find three people positively impacted by your brand.
8. Share your story. Revise it. Share again.

PR Superpower 1 — Wow Storytelling Superpower

Once you implement these Wow Storytelling Superpower steps, your brand should inspire others to write a story about you and/or buy your product.

So, how are you feeling about your personal and business brand stories? Do they complement each other? Can you explain your top three strengths? Can you explain your mission and vision? Do you know who you can help? If you are not 100 percent sure, keep working on it. The brand story development is challenging. It will constantly evolve.

Never underestimate the power of a Wow Story that inspires others. It is the main driver for your Ultimate Media Success!

With your brand story foundation, this book will share how to gain more earned media with eight new *8-Second PR* Superpowers. It is the combination of all the PR Superpowers in this book that can make your story go really viral with fans.

Chapter 1 — 8-Second PR Challenges

As we close Chapter 1, here are your *8-Second PR* Challenges:

1. How can you get someone's attention in eight seconds?
2. How can you tell your brand story in one to two sentences?

3. What were 3 game changers in your life that led you to your ideal job?
4. What work would you do for free?
5. What are three things that describe your brand in one sentence?
6. Can you share a mission statement with a powerful meaning in eight seconds?
7. What are your three to seven key selling points?
8. When are you going to schedule time to work on enhancing your Wow Story?

Before you go to the next chapter, take a walk.

Absorb what you have read.

Write some notes.

And then turn the page to learn about more about dominating your digital domain.

Dominate Your Digital Bank to Increase Word-of-Mouth Marketing

"In the digital space, attention is like currency. We earn it. We spend it."

—BRIAN SOLIS, DIGITAL ANALYST, SPEAKER, AND AUTHOR (ENGAGE!)

D o you have ownership over your brandname.com, and all the wrong spellings of your URL? In sync with defining a Wow Story, you must dominate the digital space for your brand. If you cannot buy the .com and get your exact match name for social media accounts, pick another name. It is really that important for your Word-of-Mouth Marketing.

With 95 percent of people in North America using the internet, and 4.1 billion people online on the planet (out of 7.6 billion, Source: *Internet World Stats*, December 2017), you must make it as easy as possible for people to find your brand on all devices (computers, smartphones, tablets and more).

And with the world online, Word-of-Mouth Marketing through digital media must be a top priority. People are 90% more likely to trust and buy from a brand recommended by a friend (*Invesprco)*, and most of these recommendations take place online.

To maximize your marketing results, you must build a digital presence so raving fans become brand advocates online. These loyal customers will share your news with friends and family simply because they are so happy with your product. This type of promotion is priceless.

Let's take a closer look at how you can own your digital bank and energize your brand story online.

■ PR Superpower 2 – Digital PR Superpower

Once you have a brand name idea, the next thing you want to do is dominate your digital bank. For Ultimate Media Success, you must enhance your **Digital PR Superpower** to increase your Word-of-Mouth Marketing. You want to own your digital assets with the same superhuman strength as a superhero. Your digital bank includes a dot com URL, mobile-friendly websites, social media channels, blog names, videos, photographs, graphics, and more. If you embrace digital marketing, your content will be listed all over the first page of *Google* results when someone searches on your product's name. To get everyone talking about your brand, you must master this *8-Second PR* Superpower!

With almost everyone on social media in North America, you just cannot afford to ignore the power of digital as a marketer today. Did you know that if *Facebook* were a country, "it would be the biggest nation on earth" (*Huffington Post*)? With approximately 185 million daily active users on *Facebook* (*CNN Money*), sponsoring posts and ads on this platform is one of the most cost-effective ways to reach millions of potential customers and fans.

Here is why your Digital PR Superpower is beyond important!

■ Top 4 Brand Benefits of Social Media Marketing

Here are our top four reasons why brands must be active on social media:

1. You can get immediate feedback from fans (it's the cheapest focus group out there).
2. You will increase your Word-of-Mouth Marketing (more people buy based on friend recommendations than anything else).
3. Reporters will check to see your digital marketing influence before deciding to interview you (you will get more interviews if you have a big fan base).
4. If you master Twitter, you can even send media pitches directly to reporters in a tweet!

This digital marketing chapter could easily be an entire book. In this chapter, we will focus primarily on marketing strategy and content versus technical step-by-step processes. To learn more about the how, *Google* to find tutorial videos about how to set up a *Facebook* business account and use social media management tools to better manage *Facebook, Twitter, LinkedIn*, and more.

You can also take my Digital Marketing for Authors online class (go to GoodyPR.com), sign up for my *UCLA Extension* online course, find slides on *Goody PR*'s *SlideShare* page, and/or read other books. (For more suggestions, see the "Resources" section in the back of this book.)

Ready? Let's go through the eight action items you need to have your brand show up in the most search results.

STEP 2 ACTION ITEMS — DOMINATE YOUR DIGITAL BANK TO INCREASE WORD-OF-MOUTH MARKETING

1. Buy the URL.com that is an exact match to your brand name FIRST.
2. Secure social media usernames for at least the top three channels with an exact match (if you cannot get the name, go back to Step 1).
3. Buy a mobile-friendly WordPress "Responsive" theme website template.
4. Post clear, concise, and compelling text content with keyword hashtags.
5. Share high-quality photos that tell your brand story.
6. Create high-quality videos that represent your brand.
7. Promote before, during, and after your brand launch.
8. Be active and current to engage your audience.

PR SUPERPOWER 2 — DIGITAL PR SUPERPOWER

First, let's take a minute to emphasize why digital marketing is a must today for every marketing professional and/or person promoting a business, book or cause. While digital does not replace the importance of traditional marketing, your overall strategy must include both to maximize results. If you use only traditional marketing such as paid newspaper ads, billboards, TV placements, and brochures, it will be much harder to get noticed.

As a marketer, your job is to think differently from millions of social media users every day to ensure your message is heard and shared. Word-of-Mouth Marketing results in 5x more sales than paid media (*Invesprco*) so you cannot afford to skip this step.

Because most people do not go anywhere without their smartphones now, you cannot overlook mobile marketing campaigns either. To drive home this point, take a look at some fun facts about popular social media trends. The digital media revolution is here and changing marketing at warp speed:

■ *Socialnomics* 2018 Video Highlights

- 50 percent of the world's population is under 30 today.
- Today's college students have never licked a postal stamp.
- 53 percent of millennials would rather lose their sense of smell than their technology.
- Two-thirds of people get their news from social media.
- 90 percent of buying decisions are influenced by social media.
- By 2020, video will account for over three-fourths of mobile usage.
- More people own a mobile device than a toothbrush.
- Every second, two people join *LinkedIn*.
- The number one hashtag is #Love.

Source: Based on video by *equalman* and the book *Socialnomics* 2018 by Erik Qualman.

Because researchers have found about 65 percent of people are visual learners, your photographs, charts, and graphics are essential to your marketing success. If you do not have a good camera to take great photos and videos, it is time to invest in one and/or hire a professional photographer (more on photo tips later in this chapter).

Let's take a closer look at these digital marketing action items with case study examples.

Step 2.1 Buy the URL.com that is an Exact Match to Your Brand Name FIRST

Before you even finalize your brand name, you must go to GoDaddy.com, Namecheckr.com, Namecheck.com, or another company that sells domain names and purchase your brandname.com.

Students in my *UCLA Extension* digital marketing class often do not understand the importance of this point. When they select a new business name for their main project for the class, I insist that the exact match URL is available. If it is not for sale, they need to pick another name.

When I was thinking about this book, the first thing I did was a *Google* search for variations of "8-Second PR," and then I bought 8SecondPR.com. I also purchased 8PRSecrets.com and several other closely related URLs.

In another case, our *Goody PR* client *Warriors Heart*, discovered that WarriorsHeart.com was not available to purchase. However, the website was not live. As a result, we researched and connected them with the URL owner using the WhoIs.com directory. The *Warriors Heart* founders asked the owner if they could purchase the URL from them. After several calls and meetings, the owner was so moved that they decided to gift this .com domain to *Warriors Heart*.

For some more popular web addresses, you can often buy "premium domains" for a much higher price. While a URL at GoDaddy for one-year averages eight dollars, these domains can cost much more.

For example, I bought DailyGoody.com for $100 because I wanted to start a good news website and connect it to our GoodyAwards.com brand. I still have not launched this website but purchased the URL because the price was reasonable. Some people even buy a bank of URLs for the sole purpose of making a profit by reselling them.

> ### ■ Case Study Example – Business.com Purchased for $7.5 million
>
> In an extreme premium domain case, the Business.com URL was purchased in 1999 for $7.5 million by Jake Winebaum's *eCompanies* as a B2B (Business-to-Business) online destination. The site is still live and covers business trends and industry news for small-to-midsize growth companies. Around the time of this purchase, I worked for a startup owned by the *eCompanies* incubator (who also owned Business.com). This outrageous purchase price for the Business.com URL was always a frequent topic of conversation at our office. In July 2007, Business.com was sold to RH Donnelley for $350 million, or 47 times the $7.5 million 1999 purchase price (*TechCrunch*). Business.com was later acquired by *Purch Group* in 2016. The terms of the deal for this Carlsbad, California, company were "not disclosed."

If you do not find a way to own your brand's exact match URL, there are much easier solutions versus spending outrageous amounts of money. Your best bet really is to change your name a little so it is unique and consistent. Bottom line, you must own your brandname.com, and there are no shortcuts.

To help you dominate your digital bank, here are our top tips:

■ 8 Tips for Brand Names & Exact Match URLs

1. Change your brand name to a two-to-three-word phrase until your .com is available.
2. Avoid really long and complicated brand names (use sixth-grade vocabulary).
3. Add a number or color to the name with a meaning that adds to your story.
4. If it is for a non-profit, buy the .com and .org URLs if available.
5. Buy additional URLs with closely related spellings (example, buy GoodyAwards.com and GoodieAwards.com).
6. Avoid using confusing spellings in your domain name.
7. Avoid dashes and punctuation in your URL name.
8. Make sure your brand URL is memorable with good SEO.

One of the most important things to consider when selecting a brand name is great SEO (Search Engine Optimization). You want a unique name so your product or service is prominent in online search results. What this means is that if you pick a brand name like "Celebrate" (no joke, someone in my marketing class chose "Celebrate" for their new company name), it will get totally lost in millions of search results for that one word.

I recommended the student change the brand name to a two-to-three-word phrase. A name like "Celebrate Big Birthdays" is more unique and works much better if the URL is available. You could be even more specific by adding geography such as "Celebrate Big Birthdays LA." While you want to keep your brand name simple, it also has to be unique so your fans can find you. Make sure you get this step right!

Step 2.2 Secure Social Media Usernames for at least the Top Three Channels with an Exact Match (if you cannot get the name, go back to Step 1)

■ Skip Ahead Option – If 90% Engagement Rate

If you have a 90% or higher engagement rate on your social media accounts already and don't need any new ideas or digital marketing insights, feel free to skip ahead to Chapter 3: Write Compelling Content with Unlimited Strength to Move Readers! If you don't know your engagement rate, you probably want to keep reading.

_____

In sync with securing your brand's dot com or dot org space, you want to register the exact match usernames for at least your top three social media platforms. With 97 percent of 16-to-64-year-olds logging into at least one social media platform per month (*Sprout Social*), you must make digital marketing a priority.

If you are not actively managing your social media, someone else will be talking about your brand online. You want to be part of that conversation.

I recommend securing usernames for your *Facebook, Twitter,* and *Instagram*. There are many platforms but focus on the top three that can best reach your audience. If your social media efforts span too many sites, you will not be as effective. You want to engage as many fans as possible with authentic content, so choose carefully.

Sure, you can set up more usernames, but develop a digital strategy that connects best with your target market and key influencers. Before you even start marketing or building your website, review your options and secure social media usernames.

Social Media Channel	Marketing Benefits
Facebook	• *Facebook* is primarily for friends and family. It can be one of your best sources for Word-of-Mouth marketing leads. • *Facebook* has the largest number of users (two billion as of June 2018), so a business page and advertising budget are highly recommended for brands. • On your personal page, be careful to balance promotional and personal posts to avoid sounding like spam. • Because *Facebook* competes with *YouTube* for video views, *Facebook* promotes videos more. The platform now has 100 million hours of video watched daily (according to *Facebook*).
Instagram	• *Instagram* is the best channel for photo marketing and visual storytelling. • *Instagram* is great for people with a product to promote, and they are adding ways to make it easier for brands to sell on this platform. • 65 percent of people are visual learners with short attention spans, which makes visual marketing very effective here.

Social Media Channel	Marketing Benefits
	• *Facebook* acquired *Instagram* for $1 billion, so businesses will need an ad budget as their "pay to play" algorithm takes over this platform. • The majority of *Instagram* users are 18 to 29, which is about 60 percent of adults online (*Sprout Social*).
Twitter	• *Twitter* is great for reaching people you do not know, using @username in a tweet that notifies the user of a mention. • You can easily cross-market using keyword #hashtags because it's like an instant chat group with people with common interests. • *Twitter* #hashtags are great for event marketing because you can reach people interested in a specific topic, issue, or geography. • Reporters use *Twitter* as a major source of news and trends. • When you get a media mention, you should always tweet the story with the @username for the outlet and reporter. • 81 percent of millennials view their *Twitter* account daily (*Sprout Social*).
YouTube	• *YouTube* can help your brand's SEO (Search Engine Optimization) with video assets showing up in search results. • *YouTube* is the second biggest search engine behind *Google*—and is owned by *Google*. People search for videos that solve problems, educate, and entertain. • You can increase the video SEO if you use a custom still image, along with keywords in the title, tags, file names and description. (This is VERY important for PR and social media marketing.) • 400 hours of video are uploaded to *YouTube* per minute (*Google*). • Eight out of ten 18-to-49-year-olds watch *YouTube*.
LinkedIn	• *LinkedIn* is perfect for small businesses who are marketing B2B (business-to-business). • *LinkedIn* is great for networking with professionals in search of jobs, connections, and/or clients.

Social Media Channel	Marketing Benefits
	• *LinkedIn* provides the ability for you to post blogs (great for SEO). • *LinkedIn* was acquired by *Microsoft* and has 575 million users (*LinkedIn*). • 25 percent of adults in the U.S. are on *LinkedIn* (*Pew Research Center*). • The site attracts people with higher paying jobs with 45 percent earning over $75,000 (*Pew Research Center*).
Snapchat	• Over 100 million people use *Snapchat* every day. • *Snapchat*'s core user base is 18 to 24 (as of January 2018). • Most pictures and messages are available for only a short amount of time (why many teens like *Snapchat*). • 60 percent of *Snapchat* users are under 25, 26 percent are 25 to 34, and 12 percent are 35 to 54 (*Hootsuite*). • 23 percent of *Snapchat* users have not graduated from high school (*Hootsuite*).
Pinterest	• Only 29 percent of adults in the U.S. use *Pinterest* (*Sprout Social*). • *Pinterest* is great for posting photos in albums with themes. For example, inspirational quotations and great Italian food can be album names that drive traffic to your page (if relevant). • *Pinterest* also lets you pin news stories as posts that can show up in Google search results. • 40 percent of *Pinterest* users have a household income of $100,000+ (*Pinterest*). • The most popular pin/photo categories include art, art supplies, and hobbies followed by flowers, food, drinks, and gifts (*Statista*).

Now that you have reviewed your social media platform options and chosen your top three social media sites, go secure the username for each one. To make your marketing easier to manage, I recommend using one consistent email for all social media accounts connected to a brand.

If someone owns your brand name's exact match on a social media channel, check to see if the account is active. If it has not posted recently, you may be able to contact the owner and ask if they are willing to transfer the ownership to you. (This transfer of ownership is a long shot and is not recommended.)

If you cannot secure your top three social media names, our recommendation is to consider changing your brand name completely until you find something where you can dominate the URL.com and social media space. Yes, this digital marketing setup process is a pain, but it is really important for branding to reach the 95 percent of internet users in the U.S.

Bottom line, you always want to be smart and consistent in your digital marketing to make it really easy for customers to find you. If someone has a hard time finding your brand online, the majority will give up quickly (remember, the average attention span for adults is eight seconds).

Let's take a closer look now at some mega names and small business brand examples to see how well they dominate their digital banks. You will notice that the mega brands are much better at consistency compared to some small businesses. Using different social media names to "make it work" rather than "make it easy for customers" is not a good idea.

MEGA BRAND EXAMPLES – DIGITAL BANK OWNERSHIP

Amazon – PERFECTLY CONSISTENT!

URL: Amazon.com
Facebook: facebook.com/amazon
Instagram: instagram.com/amazon
Twitter: twitter.com/amazon
YouTube: youtube.com/amazon

Sesame Street – MORE PERFECTION!

URL: sesamestreet.org
Facebook: facebook.com/SesameStreet
Instagram: instagram.com/sesamestreet
Twitter: twitter.com/seasamestreet
YouTube: youtube.com/sesamestreet

UGG – Not Exactly!

URL: ugg.com

Facebook: facebook.com/UGG

Instagram: instagram.com/ugg

Twitter: twitter.com/ugg

YouTube: youtube.com/user/uggaustralia — INCONSISTENT

SMALL BUSINESS EXAMPLES – DIGITAL BANK OWNERSHIP

Peet's Coffee

URL: peets.com

Facebook: facebook.com/peets

Instagram: instagram.com/peetscoffee — INCONSISTENT

Twitter: twitter.com/PeetsCoffee — INCONSISTENT

YouTube: youtube.com/channel/UChtMUHysfGfTPiWieYJY65g — INCONSISTENT
(You need 100 subscribers now to own your YouTube URL.)

Mel's Drive-In

URL: melsdrive-in.com — DASH IN URL

Facebook: https://www.facebook.com/MelsDriveInSunset — INCONSISTENT

Instagram: instagram.com/melsdrivein

Twitter: twitter.om/MelsDriveIn

YouTube: No YouTube Channel

Fruit Bliss

URL: fruitbliss.com

Facebook: facebook.com/fruitbliss

Instagram: Instagram.com/fruit_bliss — UNDERSCORE in NAME

Twitter: twitter.com/fruit_bliss — UNDERSCORE in NAME

YouTube: youtube.com/channel/UCDTb_DphrOHGCS60joFEtgg
(Fruit Bliss Snacks)

Step 2.3 Buy a Mobile-Friendly WordPress "Responsive" Theme Website Template

When you build a website, we recommend using a "responsive" *WordPress* theme template that is mobile-ready for the best SEO. You may also try another option like *WIX Mobile Site Builder*. We prefer *WordPress* because it offers great SEO. Your job is to get as many eyeballs on your brand as possible so pay attention to what tools work best for optimizing your search results.

A "responsive" theme is a must because it is mobile-friendly, which means it adjusts to fit the size of your device screen (computer, smartphone, and tablet). It's so important that *Google* will now lower your website in the search engines if you are not mobile-friendly. Search online for the themes that say "responsive" and pay the low fee. It is so worth it!

For an example of a *WordPress* template, *Google* the Montana template by *ThemeForest* or "best *WordPress* responsive themes." You will pay a little for these templates, but it is usually a minimal one-time fee (around $17 to $59). The Montana template design is simple and has many customization options for the menu and layout. When you are reviewing options, look for the "Live Preview" button to view an actual website built using the template.

> ### ■ Mobile Website Case Study - TheMichaelBlank.com
>
> To see a really impressive mobile website for a small business owner, check out themichaelblank.com. As an author, mentor, coach, and real estate investor who specializes in apartment building investing, Michael Blank's website is easy to navigate, and the graphics, photographs, and videos speak volumes about his brand. The overall content conveys confidence in Blank as the author of "Financial Freedom with Real Estate Investing" and leading authority on apartment building investing. This digital presence has contributed to this CEO raising millions of dollars for multi-family investments.

For our GoodyPR.com website update in April 2018, we chose the Noho template by *ThemeForest*. We like the clean design with a video prominently displayed on the home page. The video highlights a recent TV interview for one of our client's, which is important for any public relations company. We also LOVE the Portfolio page that showcases examples of our work with pictures, video, and descriptions. The Services page includes graphics and a simple design to display a menu of options for clients.

However, once we bought the Noho theme template, it did not look exactly like the online "Live Preview" website. As a result, one of our *Goody PR* developers customized it. As a team, we spent a few weeks going back and forth fine-tuning the format to match our "Let us Magnify Your Good" tag line and brand.

Even if you are very familiar with *WordPress*, we still recommend hiring a developer to help you with the behind-the-scenes technical pieces. For example, our developer contacted the *WordPress* Noho template designer through online help to find ways to customize the website better.

There are also *WordPress* plug-ins you will need. Plug-ins are used for security, *Google Analytics*, connecting to your social media channels, social sharing, spam prevention, and other functions that make your website more efficient. Unless you are a developer, hire the pros to take care of these details.

To be more efficient, we highly recommend hiring a website developer based in the U.S. for anything complex. While you might think you are saving a lot of money by hiring someone overseas, you may actually spend more in both your time and dollars in the end.

For example, when we were developing the GoodyAwards.com website, an overseas developer was taking weeks to figure out the online voting system. The challenge was that the coding for the voting system was very complicated. It needed to be integrated with *Twitter* and automatically count hashtags. For example, a tweet with #HeroGoody equaled one vote. The system integration was not working. After almost three weeks with no success, we switched to a highly recommended developer in Los Angeles. In less than an hour, the new guy had the *Goody Awards* voting system working with Twitter.

It may also be helpful to use a project management software system to keep your website content and updates in a central place online. For example, when working at *Fox Interactive Media/Myspace*, we used *BaseCamp* to manage complex projects across departments. *Goody PR* has since used *BaseCamp* to manage big projects for clients with multiple team members in different locations.

Along with choosing a website template, here is a quick summary checklist of what you need to build your brand website.

Must Haves for Branded Website	Why
Buy URL from GoDaddy or Another Site	Buy your exact match dot com URL, and pay an annual fee before doing anything else when launching a brand.
Purchase your Responsive *WordPress* Theme or Template	Buy a responsive website theme that is mobile friendly. Buy a template as a starting point for a one-time fee of about $49 (average), and then hire a developer to help you with customizations.
Set up Hosting with a Company	You will also need someone to host your website (*GoDaddy, HostGator*, and other sites). Hosting usually requires an annual fee and may include extra fees for custom email (Example: yournameATwebsite.com). Ask a lot of questions and get recommendations for hosting.
SSL or Secure URL	If you are selling products online, you should also purchase an SSL (Secure Sockets Layer) certificate so your website is secure with https. SSL can also help your SEO rankings.
Google Analytics	You should also set up *Google Analytics* so you can track your website traffic. (*Google* setup instructions are online.)
Plug-Ins	Plug-ins are like apps for websites (there are many). You can add website plug-ins to your administration portal for many reasons. Your best bet is to hire a developer who can recommend and install plug-ins based on your needs. Plug-ins are added to the website in the back-end administration portal on *WordPress*.

Must Haves for Branded Website	Why
Company Logo and Creative Assets	You will also need your company logo and creative assets (images and photos) ready for a website. If you do not have this creative, you can always hire a graphic designer. I recommend hiring a professional designer for logos. The cost can range anywhere from $800 to $20,000 for major brands. If you have a low budget, try Fiverr.com or a website where contractors can compete for the job online.
Site Map and Content	You will also need to draft a site map that lists all the pages in your website menu, along with your creative assets or content (text, images, video).

Now that you have purchased your dot com for your brand name, secured your top three social media site usernames, and launched your website, it is time to start posting compelling content online.

Step 2.4 Post Clear, Concise, and Compelling Text Content with Keyword Hashtags

Similar to a great press release, media pitch, or keynote address, your online content must immediately grab the reader's attention. For branding, consistency is also essential in your digital marketing.

SEO STRATEGY IS YOUR NEXT PRE-LAUNCH STEP

When you post your content, you need a great SEO strategy first. Your digital marketing text determines whether people can find you online. For the best results, make sure you have a keyword strategy upfront.

You want to identify the phrases and/or keywords that you will use over and over again to direct your desired target audience traffic to your brand. This list of keywords should be used consistently in social media text posts, image names, photo names, video file names, and blogs to get the best results.

Choose one key hashtag for your product, service, or book to use with every social media post. For example, for the new book *He Started It!: My Twitter War with Trump*, the team chose #HeStartedIt as the primary hashtag. Yes, this is a competitive phrase, but since the author owns HeStartedIt.com and it is the book title, it worked. We also used keyword hashtags such as the author name #DannyZuker, his job at #ModernFamily, and the category #PoliticalHumorBook.

Your brand's keywords are important for all digital content. How many times have you gone to *YouTube* to search for a video and could not find it? Chances are the person who posted the video forgot to put keywords in the title, description, and/or video tags. It always amazes us that some marketers do not understand why the text and tags are so important.

■ Case Study Example – *Goody Awards* Video Keywords

As a video success story example, we posted a *Goody Awards* interview that surprisingly went viral on *YouTube*. It was an interview with a Holocaust survivor who was one of 669 children saved by Sir Nicholas Winton during World War II.

While Sir Nicholas Winton was world-famous, and was featured on *60 Minutes*, this video interview with child-survivor Dave Lux consistently landed on the top of page one of *YouTube* search results for "Sir Nicholas Winton" and "child survivor."

We filmed this 84-year-old survivor during a light rain in Los Angeles in his backyard with a nice camera (but not a crew or fancy lights). This 2013 video now has more than 153,000+ views (November 2018)! It is a really moving story about the day Dave Lux met the man who saved his life. His story plus the SEO keywords made the big difference in getting so many views!

For all SEO, it is best to use keyword phrases rather than single words because there is way too much competition for individual words on *Google*. The more specific you are, the more likely you will be found online. In this case, the keywords "child survivor," "Sir Nicholas Winton," "Dave Lux," and "World War II" were all included in the video tags on *YouTube*.

Another good SEO example is instead of using a single word like "restaurant" as the keyword, use a phrase like "best sushi restaurant Los Angeles." By adding the food type and geography, you can attract your target audience much faster. Here are some more SEO keyword examples as a quick snapshot:

Mega Brand	Bad SEO Keywords	Much Better SEO Keywords
Airbnb	Vacation	"economy travel" "cheap hotel los angeles"
Apartment Therapy	Apartments	"home décor and design" "how to update your home" and "new york"
Etsy	Jewelry	"handmade necklace" "custom jewelry designs Miami"
Wayfair	Homes	"home decorating design firm" "best home furnishings"
All Recipes	Recipes	"best low carb recipes" "best gluten free recipes"

We cannot emphasize enough the importance of using your SEO keywords everywhere in your digital assets, including blog posts, website URLs, press releases, columns, blogs, videos, image names, and social media posts.

WRITE CLEAR MESSAGES ON SOCIAL MEDIA POSTS

Your next step is to write clear messages on *Facebook, Twitter, Instagram, LinkedIn* and more, which is much easier said than done. No one wants to read a really long social media post or be left guessing what you meant. Your challenge is to make what you are saying obvious with as few words as possible.

If you are not sure if your content makes sense, ask a friend for HONEST feedback before posting. You can also do A/B testing. This approach is done all the time in advertising. Simply post two to three different versions of your message on social media to see which one gets the best response.

No matter what type of content you are selling or promoting, you need to be clear in your first one to two sentences. Remember, you have only eight seconds to get their attention!

To engage users, it is best to ask a question. You can also include a "Call to Action" to guide readers towards what you want them to do (buy, comment, donate, check it out).

Let's look at some examples of photo descriptions posted on Instagram.

Original Instagram Post	Much Clearer Instagram Post
This week on #TheNightTimeShow Podcast @mikeblackattack @funnymatt and I interviewed world famous provocateur/photographer @thetylershields about..... 1. The Kathy Griffin situation 2. Ryan Kavanaugh's blood doctor 3. Lindsay Lohan 4. The FBI in his house 5. My stupid jacket 6. Heather Morris Death Threats 7. Shooting on film 8. POSTMATES POISON 9. Suge Knight music video with Tupac 10. Blood party Listen to the show by clicking the link in my bio	Check out our fun & timely #TheNightTimeShow Podcast @mikeblackattack @funnymatt interview with world famous photographer @thetylershields RE: 1. #KathyGriffin situation 2. #LindsayLohan 3. How to take photos of #headlinenews topics 4. Plus more LOLs – just posted. LISTEN by clicking iTunes link in my bio.
This custom home has some very luxurious, yet unique interior design. Question is are you loving it? Or leaving it?. Iconic residence situated in prestigious Bayview village. This home is the pinnacle of perfection with 7" wide rift-cut white oak hardwood flooring throughout main & 2nd floor. Custom quality designer kitchen cabinetry with double island & server area and a marble counter top & back splashes. The family room ceiling was designed with exotic wood. Temperature-control wine cellar, all wolf/subzero/mile appliances. Approx. 5,000 sq. ft on the main & second floors plus 2,800 sq. ft in the basement.	Are you looking for the perfect luxury home in Toronto, Ontario? This "Pinnacle of Perfection" is waiting for you! 8 THINGS TO LOVE: 1. 7"-wide rift-cut white oak hardwood flooring throughout main & 2nd floor 2. Custom quality designer kitchen cabinetry with double island & server area with marble counter top & back splashes. 3. Temperature-control wine cellar, all wolf/subzero/mile appliances 4. Gym with steam sauna. 5. Two laundry rooms with Samsung Washer & Dryer 6. Home theatre

Original Instagram Post	Much Clearer Instagram Post
Other features include Crestron smart system with two 10" touch screens. Lenox WIFI thermostat. Two high efficiency Lenox hvac system. Two laundry rooms with two sets of Samsung washer & dryer. Gym with steam sauna, designated home theatre. Elevator with mirror & wall paper. Location: 27 FLAREMORE CRESCENT #Toronto, Ontario Price: $4,788,000 CAD Bedrooms: 5+1 Bathrooms: 9 5,000 Sq ft Listed by Arash Vakili @rightathomerealty Photos by RealMedia.ca #the6 #the6ix #curbappeal #propertygrams #luxuryhomes #realestate #dreamhome #luxuryinterior #customhome Turn on our post notifications on our Instagram page @propertygrams and subscribe to our YouTube channel (Link in Bio)	7. Elevator with mirror & wall paper 8. Approx. 5,000 square feet on main & second floors plus 2,800 square feet in the basement. Location: 27 FLAREMORE CRESCENT #Toronto, Ontario Price: $4,788,000 CAD Bedrooms: 5+1 Bathrooms: 9 5,000 Sq ft Interested? Contact: Arash Vakili @rightathomerealty Photos by RealMedia.ca #the6 #the6ix #curbappeal #propertygrams #luxuryhomes #realestate #dreamhome #luxuryinterior #customhome

WRITE CONCISE MESSAGES

While you may think it is easy to be clear and concise, it's not. For example, we brainstorm potential media topics with new clients to learn about their products and services. In one case, a new client recommended, "Listen to my hundreds of podcasts (one hour each) to figure out which media topics to pitch about me." Really? No one has time to listen to hours of content to figure out what your brand means. If you cannot explain your brand story in a few sentences or a one-page summary with bullets and photos, you can forget about winning over the media, fans, and influencers!

To market your book, product, or service, you must grab your audience's attention immediately. If they are confused upfront, you may have lost them, and maybe forever!

Twitter is our favorite social media site for concise messages. Despite their 240-character limit per tweet, many posts could be much clearer and moving. Take a look at these tweet comparisons.

Original Twitter Message	Clearer Twitter Message
Increasingly, I have noticed entrepreneurs talking about "disrupting" industries as a primary objective and not just an effect of their innovation. Here is why I think it is time to start talking about solutions and building companies again.	Have you noticed many entrepreneurs talk more about "disrupting" industries versus actually taking action? Let's start talking about solutions.
An impressionistic artist who works mainly with a palette knife and oils. He has his own unique technique & style which is unmistakable & cannot be confused with other artists. His paintings usually reflect certain personal memories and emotions	Calling #ArtLovers! Check out this #ImpressionisticArtist who works mainly with a #paletteknife & oils. LOVE his unique technique & style that draws out so many emotions!
Social Media Contest! Enter your photo or video with Stop Selling & Start Leading book to win free #sales coaching from @PeopleFirstPS. Use the hashtag #ExtraordinatrySales to post your photo on Instagram, Facebook, LinkedIn or Twitter.	Say CHEESE to Win 1-hr #SalesCoaching with @PeopleFirstPS pros & increase revenues! 2 easy steps: 1. Post photo/video of you with "Stop Selling & Start Leading" book 2. Include #ExtraordinarySales in your posts on Facebook, Instagram, LinkedIn or Twitter

WRITE COMPELLING CONTENT THAT CONNECTS

Compelling content is simply an authentic message from the heart that emotionally moves the reader. If you do not inspire fans, you will get low engagement (likes, shares, comments, views, or responses to your Call To Action). As a marketing person, your goal should always be to move people to increase responses and revenue. If your audience is not thinking "wow, incredible, so inspiring, very helpful, or fantastic," they are probably skimming over your website and social media.

We highly recommend using emphasis phrases to focus on your one "most important thing" or "top three things." This *8-Second PR* **"Bold Statements Strategy"** also applies to every type of communication about a brand online and offline (interviews, videos, photos, blogs, speaking events and more).

Let's take a closer look at a few *Facebook* posts and see how you can make your content more interesting. Focus on sounding humble and balanced online. You want to avoid turning people off. People who only post long-winded text and photos of themselves online can get really boring fast. Remember, giving thanks, showing compassion and sharing interesting stories go a long way in many facets of life, especially online.

LONG Facebook Message	More Clear, Concise & Compelling Facebook Messages
These two babies are 17 and 19 years old in this picture. It is 2004 - she's about to graduate high school, and he's about to transfer to a new college in the Fall. It is not the right time to start dating, it is just a summer love, they tell themselves. These two have no idea in this moment that they will not only make it through that summer, but through 4 years of college long-distance, they will move out to Los Angeles together, they'll get engaged, get married (and have the most fun wedding!), travel all over the world, and become parents	This is my favorite photo with my true love, and always reminds me to be grateful! We were just babies at 17 & 19 years. It is 2004 – she's about to graduate from high school & he's about to transfer to a new college in the Fall. It is not the right time to start dating, it is just a summer love – so they tell themselves...And NOW, 14 years later, we are happily married for 5 years with a beautiful daughter and great life. Thank you for this beautiful journey my love - cannot wait for more!

LONG Facebook Message	More Clear, Concise & Compelling Facebook Messages
to a daughter, and soon move in to their first home together. They have no idea what they are in for, they have no idea how much they will mean to one another. In this moment, he's just a cute baseball player with nice blue eyes. They'll see. Happy 5 years married // 14 years together.	
Win a unique & hand-crafted Wood American Flag! The quality of these flags matches the quality of healing that went into the construction of it through *Warriors Heart Foundation* Three ways to get one ($5 each or 3/$10): 1. Let us know how many you would like and we will send a picture of your tickets here on Facebook (donations here: Facebook page. ((If someone wins that is not local, flag can be mailed +postage)) 2. In person before *Liberty Day* (we will always have some with us) 3. At the *Warriors Heart Foundation* display in front of the Old Courthouse at the Columbiana Liberty Day	Win a unique, hand-crafted wooden American Flag!* You can win a one-of-a-kind custom American Flag and help heal our protectors by buying a raffle ticket for $5 or entering the Silent Auction benefiting *Warriors Heart Foundation*. This handmade flag was made by warriors (military, veterans and first responders) at *Warriors Heart* to "pay it forward" by raising funds to heal fellow warriors struggling with addiction and PTSD. 1. Raffle drawing and Silent Auction is June 30 (at *Liberty Day Festival* in Alabama). Buy tickets: Facebook page. 2. Your purchase is a donation to WarriorsHeartFoundation. org 3. *Warriors Heart Foundation* supplements insurance costs not covered for residential treatment at Warriors Heart.

*If winner is not local, flag can be mailed +postage

Step 2.5 Share High-Quality Photos that tell Your Brand Story

High-quality photos are one of the most important parts of any digital marketing strategy, and one of the easiest ways to tell a story in eight seconds. This is one of my favorite topics, and I could write a whole book about photo and video marketing. I am so passionate about photography that I had a dark room in our basement at age 17, own five cameras, and literally almost married someone because of the dark room in his home (no joke!).

According to *Forbes*, content with visuals receive 94 percent more views, so you should ALWAYS post online with photos or video.

While everyone has suddenly become a photographer with a smartphone, it is much better to take important photos with a real digital camera. You can get away with a smartphone photo for social media, but for a website, marketing materials or media story, the pros usually insist on high-quality images.

For example, when the *Chicago Tribune* asked for photos as options for a book review story for our client, they chose an author photo we took with a *Nikon COOLPIX P7700 Digital Camera*. The reporter was given ten photo options that included the book cover, author headshots, and photos taken backstage before a TV interview. Images were taken with an iPhone and this professional camera. The major newspaper team chose the *Nikon* image because it was high quality (2MB), had good lighting, and the author was holding up their book. They insisted on crediting our name and company (which was great cross-marketing for *Goody PR* and the author).

Never underestimate the power of photos for energizing your brand story. If you think "everyone" can take great pictures and the camera does not matter, you are missing a major PR opportunity.

Here are some interesting *Instagram* statistics as of January 2018 to drive home the importance of marketing with pictures.

> **■ *Instagram* Warp Speed Growth Makes Photo Marketing a Top Priority!**
>
> - *Instagram* has over 800 million active monthly users, and many estimate that the number of monthly users will grow to one billion in 2018.
> - *Instagram*'s daily usage is more than double the number of *Twitter*'s.
> - An estimated 71 percent of businesses in the U.S. use *Instagram*.

- Eighty percent of users follow a business on *Instagram*.
- At least 30 percent of *Instagram* users have purchased a product they discovered on *Instagram*.
- Posts with a location get 79 percent more engagement.
- Seventy percent of *Instagram* posts are not seen because of a new algorithm (secret formula for what gets seen) by *Facebook* (who owns Instagram).
- Instagram users engage more on weekdays (Tuesday to Friday, 9 a.m. to 6 p.m. are the best times to post).
- Instagram photos get 36 percent more engagement than videos.
- Photos with faces get 38 percent more likes.
- 59 percent of 18-to-29-year-olds use Instagram.
- 80 percent of *Instagram* users live outside the U.S.

Source: *Sprout Social* (Feb 12, 2018)
18 *Instagram* Stats Every Marketer Should Know for 2018

Are you now inspired to post more high-quality photos and have a photo marketing strategy? Let's talk about how to take WOW Photos to capture your audience's attention.

Along with owning five cameras, I took a photography class at the *Corcoran School of Art* in Washington D.C. to learn photography styles and strategies. All of my photos were black and white for this class (love black and white!). The hours spent in the dark room were endless because of our love for photo art. Here are our top eight Wow Photo Tips for how to make people look twice.

■ *8-Second PR* Wow Photo Tips

1. BUY A GOOD CAMERA — Quality photos matter so much on social media that it is really worth buying a good camera. You do not have to spend a fortune because the cost of many digital cameras is cheaper than an iPhone. Our favorite camera is a *Canon Powershot* with a 60x zoom. The quality of the close-up photos and video is so good that I have bought this camera three times over the past seven years. The only drawback is that the photo quality wears out if you use the zoom a lot (which we do).

2. TELL A STORY — Take photos that tell a story that moves people. I learned this strategy listening to *National Geographic* photographer Dave Yoder speak at an event in Los Angeles. Yoder

spent six months at the Vatican in Rome, Italy, to get the perfect photo of the Pope that told a story. Think about the message in your story, and pay attention to the details—the expressions, colors, content, lighting, composition (layout), and more.

3. FIND GOOD LIGHTING — Move around until you get the best lighting, inside and outside. Do not be afraid to ask people to shift places and/or even go to another location to get this right. Most people do not mind moving if you tell them it will make them look good! To see examples, compare the lighting quality on TV by flipping cable news channels covering the same event. Some producers have told us, "It is all about the lighting on TV!" You can also check out our Instagram @LizHKelly for examples. Lighting is paramount in your pictures and videos!

4. WATCH BACKGROUNDS — Pay attention to the background so nothing odd is sticking out of someone's head! A tree or pole can be really distracting if it is in the wrong place in your photo. (So many people miss this detail!)

5. RULE OF THIRDS — Use the rule of thirds when taking photos. Line up the horizon and subject with the grid lines on your smartphone or camera. Avoid having your subject in the center. It is much better to place your subject to the right or left side as *60 Minutes* does in TV interviews. Google to find visual examples of this rule online.

6. TRY DIFFERENT ANGLES — Move your camera and body around to take different angles. We learned this tip from Marc Karzen when we first moved to Los Angeles. Marc studied photography at the *Sorbonne* in Paris and later did graphics for *Saturday Night Live* and *Late Night with David Letterman*. He recommended taking photos from a different perspective (above, below, to the side) to have images stand out. Your job is to break through the noise online, so get creative with photo storytelling!

7. LOOK FOR S CURVES — Photos with an S curve help draw attention and create a more positive visual. Pay attention to sidewalks, paths, streets, and buildings with curves. You can also direct someone's attention by slanting your camera when taking photos. We love to do turn the camera to an unexpected angle, and have seen *CNN* do this with set background images.

8. MAKE EVERYONE LOOK GOOD — Our rule is only post photos online that make everyone look good. You will win a lot more likes, shares, and comments by thinking about how everyone looks in a photo! Even if you look great, do not post a photo that makes others look really bad (unless it's your only photo of a monumental moment).

As a bonus tip, add energy to a photo with surprising expressions or motions. Try pointing up, jumping, and/or dramatically placing your arms to add emphasis in photos.

By now, you should be inspired to take great photos and know how—or know what to look for when evaluating photographers you may hire.

The final step is to confirm your brand photo strategy on social media. What are your company's colors? What types of photos will convey your brand messages the best? How often, when, and where are you going to post photos? What is your keyword strategy?

Let's take a closer look at three examples of major brands recognized for posting rock star photos on *Instagram*:

Brand Rock Star Photos on *Instagram*	Why These Brand Story Photos Stand Out
Instagram.com/ Adidas 21 million followers "Impossible is Nothing"	*ADIDAS* posts moving photos of celebrities, artists, and their sports products. For example, they have a close-up photo of *GRAMMY* winner Pharrell performing live at a Los Angeles event wearing their gear. They also have a lot of outdoor action photos that are spectacular. You will find sunset shots with runner silhouettes, along with game-day photos. These photos support their brand tag line, "Impossible is Nothing."
Instagram.com/Oreo 2.4 million followers "Milk's Favorite Cookie"	*OREO*'s *Instagram* has fun photos that tell a story. They consistently use their brand's blue and white colors and packaging. Every post includes an *Oreo* cookie, which is recognized worldwide. They also keep-it-simple, and post *Oreo* graphics and artwork. The photos all go with *Oreo*'s tag line, "Milk's Favorite Cookie."
Instagram.com/ LivingSpaces 112,000 followers* "Invent Yourself, Reshape The World"	*LIVING SPACES* posts inviting photos of comfortable rooms filled with their furniture. These photos feature complementary products that can give their customers ideas on how to use multiple products, so it is great cross-marketing!

Brand Rock Star Photos on *Instagram*	Why These Brand Story Photos Stand Out
	All photos are high-quality with excellent lighting (so important!), and the photos all support their *Living Spaces* tag line, "Invent Yourself, Reshape The World."

*Fewer followers probably because there are no people in photos.

My last photo tip for you is one that I learned at the *Corcoran School of Art*. My secret sauce for taking awesome photos is to take a TON of photos! The teacher taught us to take about 100 photos to get five great images. While I can now get about 30 great photos out of 100, I have had years of practice.

Many people think it is really easy to take great photos, and while your job is to make it look easy, it is not. For the *Hollywood Literary Retreat* in Los Angeles, we worked on their social media marketing for this annual event a few times. For one event, we arrived late due to a travel conflict. We took about 30 photos in the last hour, and their founder Lynn Isenberg said "your photos saved the day." Lynn added that the photographer who they hired did not deliver any images that could be used in their media coverage.

Most people do not realize the time involved in editing photos either. Many times, we spend five hours editing a batch of photos after a corporate event. Clients will often say, "Just send all the photos." Clearly, these comments suggest they do not have a clue about this process. And that is okay because marketing professionals and photographers are paid to tell the brand story and make it look easy.

We prefer to hire photographers for client jobs now and have several that *Goody PR* highly recommends in the Southern California area.

If you post other people's photos on social media or a website, make sure to credit them properly and/or ask for permission. Some images may also be copyrighted and require you to pay a fee to republish them. There are also websites where you can buy stock and celebrity photos.

Along with professional photos, you can post more casual smartphone photos because imperfect images can come across as more authentic marketing. Edit your photos with apps and filters to make your images stand out more online.

Liz H. Kelly

You will find recommendations for photo apps in the "Resources" section in the back of this book.

Do not forget the power of infographics either! These informational graphics have shown the greatest increase in usage for B2B marketers in the past four years—now 65 percent, according to the *Content Marketing Institute*.

Have a blast taking photos, post daily on social media with consistent hashtags, and/or hire a professional to enhance your visual storytelling.

> ### ■ *8-Second PR* Storytelling Photo Tip
>
> The bottom line is that you can tell a powerful story with a photograph in eight seconds - making photographs one of your most important digital marketing assets.

Pay careful attention to the strategy, story, and content. We are still talking about marketing here—right? Did you almost forget? It is easy to get side-tracked when you are having fun talking about photos!

Step 2.6 Create High-Quality Videos that Represent Your Brand

Did you know that most people decide whether to continue watching a video within the first fifteen seconds? You must immediately capture your audience's attention based on the quality of the video's visual, sound and content.

Posting a great versus good video for your brand is an art. While some poor-quality videos taken with a smartphone go viral, your brand will be much better represented by a professionally made production. The video must include many greats—a moving story, clear and consistent messaging, great lighting, great composition, graphics that complement the story, great editing, and potentially background music—that all match your brand message.

For example, the *Goody Awards YouTube* Channel was started in 2012. Six years later, this channel has almost six million video views, 3,000 subscribers, and over 310 videos (as of November 2018). *YouTube* also has analytics reports so you can see what videos are getting the most views and comments. These *YouTube* reports provide great insights for marketers, including the sites and geography where people are watching. You can even see when viewers drop off and people stop watching your videos.

Our biggest *Goody Awards YouTube* win is a *Hunger Games* cast video, which includes Jennifer Lawrence, Josh Hutcherson, Liam Hemsworth, and Lenny Kravitz at the *San Diego Comic-Con International* in 2013. There are several reasons this *Goody Awards* video went viral and has almost ONE MILLION VIEWS. Yes, it helped to have celebrities in it, but many others took videos of the same panel—here is why this video worked so well:

■ *Goody Awards YouTube* **Channel Case Study:**
Why *Hunger Games* Cast Video Got Almost One Million Views

---

1. MATCH YOUR TARGET AUDIENCE — Our *Goody Awards* audience is mostly teens and people who want to change the world. In the *Hunger Games* movie series with Jennifer Lawrence as the lead protagonist, there are many women-empowerment messages that also matched the interests of our core demographic.

2. EDIT TO TELL A STORY — In this four-minute video, we pulled out the best stories from the panel. When Josh Hutchinson and Jennifer Lawrence started describing the time they filmed their kissing scenes in bad weather and how snot was coming out of Jennifer's nose, all while laughing hysterically, we knew this moment was the video gold in this 45-minute panel!

3. FUNNY = MONEY — Humor, of course, goes a long way with videos. I like to emphasize "Funny = Money" in my digital marketing class. For this video, Jennifer and Josh were laughing so hard while describing their "Snot Kisses". You could also see the genuine audience reaction to this hilarious conversation.

4. VIDEO QUALITY MATTERS — My *Canon Powershot* 50x zoom camera made the video look almost like TV quality. Watching this video, you would never know the reality was that I was filming in a sea of 6,500 people crammed into the *San Diego Convention Center* Hall H. The farther you zoom when filming video or taking photos, the harder it is to hold the camera still. To keep a steady hand, I often use a monopole. I even held my breath a few times so my breathing would not make the camera move. It's far from perfect, but looks pretty good.

5. VIDEO COMPOSITION — Where you place the camera angle also matters. I was fortunate to get an aisle seat in the center. *Comic-Con* lets the media stand to the side for filming, but those views are not nearly as good as from where our group sat. This center

---

angle put me in the perfect location for video filming. I owe this placement to my unsung hero, Ting Lei, who literally slept outside the *San Diego Convention Center* all night so we could get a great seat for this mega movie panel and others. The line is notorious for being miles long with fans trying to get into Hall H to see the biggest stars.

6. LIGHTING MATTERS — I was also fortunate that the lighting was good. My *Canon* camera is great for low light, which made a big difference in a darkened room. Similar to photographs, lighting is very important for video. Most movie productions spend a fortune on lighting for this reason.

7. SEO, OF COURSE — The SEO for this video post was a key factor in its success. We spent a lot of time getting it right—selecting the best photo for the main video image and including keywords in the video title, comprehensive description, and tags.

8. VIDEO TITLE — The video title also had great energy and stood out as different. The title for our top-ever video is "Jennifer Lawrence Kisses at *Comic-Con* Hunger Games."

To give you more examples, here are a few of my favorite viral videos that you can Google:

■ Viral Video Brand Examples

Old Spice | The Man Your Man Could Smell Like

Adele Carpool Karaoke with James Corden

Dove Real Beauty Sketches | You are more beautiful than you think (3 minutes)

Susan Boyle audition - Britain's Got Talent

Superman with a GoPro

Avicii - Feeling Good

David After Dentist

During my digital marketing class, students are required to make a two-to-three-minute video describing their new brand. The best videos include a story, many visuals (graphics, titles, photo images), and enthusiasm by the student (who is acting as a CEO of their new brand). It is a great exercise and much harder than you would think. If you had to create a two-to-three-minute video about your brand, how would you tell the story?

■ Create a VIDEO of You Telling Your Brand Story

For book marketing and PR, you need a short 2-3-minute video of you talking about your brand story that must be both educational and entertaining. Reporters want to see how you come across on camera before booking you for a radio or TV interview. If you don't have a video of you speaking about your brand, add that to your action item list.

You are also going to need more than one video, and one for each of your media spokespeople. Start brainstorming fun video ideas that tell a story about your brand. Sure, you can draft a script, but do not read it. You want it to sound authentic, so an outline of key talking points works great for the filming preparation. You might need multiple takes, but that is okay.

■ *Goody PR* Case Study — Book Promo Video

When our *Goody PR* author client Lynn Isenberg (*The Funeral Planner, Author Power*) asked for help filming a book promo video, we became the disruptor. Lynn is a recognized novelist, producer, and screenwriter, who is used to having a formal script. When we walked on the set, Lynn was prepared with cue cards for the talent to read for this video. After several disastrous takes, we recommended not using the cue cards to sound more natural. The results were 100 times better. It took her a few minutes to let go of the script emotionally, but it worked so much better that she was very grateful in the end. It was still the same talking points, but the actor spoke more from the heart versus a script.

Keep in mind that videos can change the world, especially the way we market our brands. What stories can you film to promote your personal or business brand?

■ *Goody PR* **Case Study — Speaker Reel Video for Tom Wheelwright**

As another *Goody PR* case study example, we worked with a professional video editor to develop a speaker reel for CPA, CEO, and tax expert, Tom Wheelwright. He was speaking in Australia, and we found a video production team in Sydney to partner with us for this project. Tom spoke on six continents that year, and the video incorporated an interview with him, along with multiple clips of him speaking on stage in different cities. Everything from the composition, sound quality, order of the clips, banner text, main video image, title, description, and keywords resulted in a great response online. This professional video raised the bar for attracting more speaking engagements, and now a Speakers Bureau has called to hire him to speak at a conference. You can see this video on *Goody PR's YouTube* Channel: "Tax and Wealth Speaker Tom Wheelwright Puts Money in Your Pocket."

Step 2.7 Promote Before, During, and After Your Brand Launch

Once you have a ton of great content, you need to decide when and how you will post it online. While some people recommend waiting until the "official launch" to promote your book, product, service, or new movie, most marketing pros today will advise posting content before, during, and after a new product goes live. You can share the content in stages leading up to a launch and include teaser campaigns. Remember, anyone who thinks a marketing campaign should only be a three-month launch blitz is missing out on months of potential sales, brand awareness, and promotions.

Why do you think the summer blockbuster movies start marketing at *Comic-Con* a year in advance of the theatrical release? Producers often premiere "sneak preview" content that is exclusive for *Comic-Con* attendees just to get people excited! The studios know the importance of building a fan base early. You always want to encourage Word-of-Mouth marketing so that fans and influencers start building buzz for you. Of course, major franchises like *The Avengers* or *Star Wars* just build off of the current fan base over and over again. However, the stars, directors, and producers continue to participate in promotions at *San Diego Comic-Con International* with 130,000+ fans in July.

■ Product Launch Case Study — *Autism Guardian Angels*

When *Goody PR* built the branding and launch plan for *Autism Guardian Angels* (new Venture Capitalist (VC) for autism technology products, aka *Shark Tank* for autism products and services), we developed an integrated marketing campaign with multiple marketing elements, outlined here:

1. Launched a mobile website before major Autism Awareness Month launch campaign.
2. Posted consistent social media posts on *Facebook, Instagram,* and *Twitter* before, during, and after the launch.
3. Launched an iPad sweepstakes to enter on *Facebook* and *Twitter* during April's Autism Awareness Month.
4. Sponsored the first *Autfest Film Festival* hosted by *the Autism Society of America*, including films made by and about autistic people.
5. Cross-marketed with the *Autism Society* before, during and after *Autfest*.
6. Wrote blogs and press releases about *Autfest* and other autism events that we attended.
7. Honored autism advocate Matt Asner with a *Golden Goody Award* (our top humanitarian *Goody Award*) "for dedicating over 20 years to raising autism awareness, helping millions impacted by autism, and as a parent of autistic children."
8. Filmed red carpet interview videos at *Autfest* with autistic filmmakers, filmmakers, and stars (Ben Affleck, *Pixar* Filmmakers) for our new *Autism Guardian Angels YouTube* Channel.

This integrated marketing campaign "put *Autism Guardian Angels* on the map," according to our *Goody PR* client who was thrilled to get so much attention within a short timeframe. This campaign not only connected with the millions impacted by autism, but it also raised awareness of this new investment fund within the tech community.

Step 2.8 Be Active and Current to Engage Your Audience

To keep your fans engaged with your content online, you want to update your brand regularly with new themes, timely messages, and relevant campaigns. Similar to your media pitches, you want to adjust based on the season, trends, and campaigns. People like "new" things, so you cannot pick just one marketing theme, and let it go. We will talk more about reinventing your brand throughout this book, and especially in Chapter 8.

The most important thing to remember about engaging fans on social media is it is a two-way conversation. It is a give-and-take. No one wants friends who make everything about themselves. Honestly, have you been to a party where one person talks non-stop about their life and never takes a breath to ask you a question? It is the same thing. Ask questions, get people engaged, and show you really care to earn fan loyalty!

If you post all day long and never LIKE anyone else's posts in return, your fans and friends will get bored and go away. Unless you are a celebrity, well-known public figure, or influencer, your popularity will not last very long online with a one-way conversation.

You want to engage with your friends on social media because it's polite. They are also your best source of Word-of-Mouth marketing. If you are not sure what type of content they like best, you can host a free focus group easily by asking for immediate feedback on *Facebook, Twitter,* or *Instagram*.

Your digital marketing strategy is not complete unless it includes ways to engage your fans. It is not enough to just post great content. People, especially influencers, often want something in return. You might offer an "exciting prize" for a sweepstakes, free products or services, and/or an experience (concert tickets, a trip, conference tickets) as a way to increase your fan engagement.

> ■ **Case Study Example –** *University of Phoenix* **Backstage Passes**
>
> While working for *Fox Interactive Media/Myspace,* the *University of Phoenix* sponsored a "Back to School Campaign" that included a 35-city tour with singer Kate Voegele (*One Tree Hill*). Kate would take classes on the bus on her laptop, and then perform at night at venues across the U.S. To keep fans engaged, Kate participated in a weekly online chat. Through a custom *Myspace* page, fans could win backstage passes and be entered into a sweepstakes for an autographed guitar. This campaign was such a huge success that the *University of Phoenix* ran it three times.

In all digital marketing, you should always be listening to fans and engaging with them online (comment, like, re-tweet). You can do it yourself and/or hire a team of professionals so the brand is consistently present.

You should also invest in social media monitoring tools ranging from free to $5,000 or more per year. Many of these tools provide valuable reporting to help you identify trends. You can see what posts are working and what content does not connect to fans. (See the "Resources" section of this book for social media management tools.)

■ Mobile Marketing Case Study — *TAO Nightclub* Campaign

Mobile marketing is another digital marketing tool that is evolving, and cannot be overlooked as we close this chapter. With users spending an average of 69 percent of their media time on smartphones (*comScore*), pay attention to this space.

As a case study example, check out this *TAO Nightclub* mobile promotion. Here's how this worked:

- 2,000 opt-in *TAO Nightclub* subscribers received an exclusive text message offer.
- 11 percent redeemed the offer.
- 220 additional attendees came to the event based on this offer.
- $1,770 revenue was generated in additional admission fees.
- $4,400 revenue was generated for additional drinks (two per person at $10 per drink).

What is consistent in mobile marketing case studies is that text message campaigns with a "special offer" work best. With over 40 percent of online transactions being made on smartphones from June to September 2017 according to *Google Analytics*, mobile marketing is gaining traction. With the right mobile campaign, it can add a significant return on investment (ROI).

Source: *30 Mobile Marketing Case Studies You Need to Know*, Tatango.com blog

---

While many are still trying to figure out how to maximize mobile marketing, B2C (business-to-consumer) brands need to pay attention to this space. One simple solution for mobile marketing is to run a *Groupon* with a special discount offer to drive traffic to your store. You can set this up easily online and then watch your sales increase.

Engagement reports and ROI (Return on Investment) numbers should be evaluated whenever you are planning a social media marketing campaign. Once you have fine-tuned your digital marketing strategy, it will get easier.

CHAPTER 2 RECAP

Are you now ready to dominate your digital footprint to increase Word-of-Mouth Marketing? Do you have a content strategy to communicate your brandname.com and social media platforms at lightning speed so everyone instantly gets what you are promoting? Marketers must master your Digital PR Superpower to win loyal fans.

Step 2 Action Items — Dominate Your Digital Bank to Increase Word-of-Mouth Marketing

1. Buy the URL.com that is an exact match to your brand name FIRST.
2. Secure social media usernames for at least the top three channels with an exact match (if you cannot get the name, go back to Step 1).
3. Buy a mobile-friendly WordPress "Responsive" theme website template.
4. Post clear, concise, and compelling text content with keyword hashtags.
5. Share high-quality photos that tell your brand story.
6. Create high-quality videos that represent your brand.
7. Promote before, during, and after your brand launch.
8. Be active and current to engage your audience.

PR Superpower 2 — Digital PR Superpower

Your Digital PR Superpower strength will impact your ability to reach a mass audience, and increase Word-of-Mouth Marketing. Your digital marketing elements must include a responsive website, compelling social media content, photographs that tell a story, viral videos and mobile marketing campaigns with a great ROI.

To continually engage fans, your digital marketing campaigns need to be creative and current with a rock solid rollout plan. When a superhero puts on their gear or gadgets, do you think they leave anything to chance? No, they triple-check that the equipment, tools, and systems are flawless.

Chapter 2 — 8-Second PR Challenges

As we close Chapter 2, here are your *8-Second PR* Challenges:

1. Are you able to secure your exact match .com and top three social media usernames for your brand?
2. What is your SEO (Search Engine Optimization) keyword strategy for your content?
3. How is your website content going to wow a fan in eight seconds?
4. What is your visual marketing strategy for photos to tell a story in eight seconds?
5. What are you going to include in the first eight seconds of your videos to engage your audience?
6. What is your 2-3 minute brand story video going to include?
7. Can you tell a powerful story in a tweet that is clear, concise and compelling?
8. What marketing elements will be in one of your digital marketing campaigns?

You will enhance your Digital PR Superpower with practice. Your best bet is to map out a calendar of digital marketing campaigns with different themes throughout the year. Start brainstorming to identify new ideas to promote your brand and do A/B testing for posts to see what content works best! Based on the feedback, continually revise your content strategy, launch new campaigns, and post new photos and videos until you get a high engagement (likes, comments, shares).

In the next chapter, we will take a closer look at writing compelling content that grabs the reader's attention.

STEP 3

Write Compelling Content with Unlimited Strength to Move Readers

---

"People do not buy goods and services. They buy relations, stories and magic."

—SETH GODIN

W hat is your favorite movie or TV show, and why? It doesn't matter if you're a Hollywood writer or a brand manager, your marketing results depend on whether people are moved by your story. Words can make or break your ultimate media success. You must write great content that emotionally connects with both your audience and reporters to succeed.

Building unlimited content strength is not easy, and will require you to be continually creative. Content is not King or Queen today. Content is the "Connector" to your audience for marketing! Most importantly, you want to write compelling stories that make people smile, scream, cry, cheer, and/or take action.

■ PR Superpower 3 – Unlimited Strength Content Superpower

Once you own your digital domain, it is time to magnify your brand story with clear, concise, and compelling content that will stand the test of time. To move readers, use the **Unlimited Strength Content Superpower** to write moving content that is unstoppable. You can gain the undivided attention of your fans by creating press releases, columns, blogs, videos, and social media posts with timely, relevant, and/or "evergreen" content. An evergreen story is a plus because it has a long shelf-life and remains fresh for years to your target market audience. Evergreen story examples include annual recaps, interviews, how-to guides, case studies, product reviews, lists (top tips), best practices, and success stories. Get ready to dig deeper into how to build lasting impressions using this *8-Second PR* Superpower.

STEP 3 ACTION ITEMS — WRITE COMPELLING CONTENT WITH UNLIMITED STRENGTH TO MOVE READERS

1. Define what you are announcing to the world.
2. Write a compelling headline with eight words or less.
3. Write a clear and concise one-sentence summary.
4. Add a quote from the heart to emphasize your message.
5. Tell a compelling story in 300 to 800 words.
6. Include credible references and statistics.
7. Choose the best press release distribution system.
8. Proofread. Test. Proofread.

PR SUPERPOWER 3 — UNLIMITED CONTENT STRENGTH SUPERPOWER

As I mentioned in the beginning of this book, one of our key strengths is a 360-degree perspective of what stories are most likely to attract earned media. This chapter will include insights based on my experiences as a marketing professional, publicist and entertainment contributor. As a way to give back and magnify good, I have written over 400 stories as a reporter for various publications. The benefit of this experience is that I better understand what the media want and need for great content.

In addition, it's important to note that as a Public Relations professional and/or industry expert, one of the fastest ways to get a story published is to offer to write great content. As the media continues to move at warp speed, more outlets are asking for story submissions. If the publication is a good match for your core demographic, there are endless opportunities for writers to get print stories published online and offline. We will talk more about targeting the right media in Chapter 5: Target Your Audience with Media Vision to Laser Focus.

The strength of every story is about how people feel after reading it.

Every story must have meaning, relevance, clarity, energy and a Call to Action. For all media, it's important to use sixth-grade vocabulary and KISS (keep it simple, stupid). The audience must get your point immediately, so remember the eight-second rule!

To help you fine-tune your message, here are our best practice tips for building great content.

Step 3.1 Define What You are Announcing to the World

When you are writing a press release, story or blog, the first thing you need to decide is what is your big announcement? You then want to define your message in one sentence because, remember, everyone is in information overload today.

Before writing anything for a new client, I usually interview them for over an hour and then brainstorm the best ways to share their message in different formats. Most CEOs and experts do not know how to tell a good story in a clear, concise, and compelling way that moves people. Business leaders are very smart people, but their genius is not always in PR. They are usually so focused on building their organization that they have a hard time stepping back and defining their Wow Story. During these client interviews, the goal is always to look for the content gold!

To define your story more clearly to the media and fans, it's best to start with the five Ws: What, Who, When, Where and Why. When you are sending a pitch to a producer or writing a story, the reader is always looking for the answers to these questions.

8-SECOND PR WS

WHAT – If you are launching a new book, your WHAT should be pretty obvious. If you are launching a company or new program, it can be more complex. If you are pitching a special segment, your "what" is the potential headline that is timely and relevant. In all cases, your job is to get to the point as quickly as possible in the first paragraph. Anytime you are announcing a new product, research finding, book or event in a press release, blog, and social media posts, it needs to go way beyond the What.

WHO – It is always best to include the WHO behind the announcement in your content. Ideally, this WHO can be a spokesperson to the media for whatever you

---

Liz H. Kelly

are telling the world. To add context or meaning, emphasize the backstory of the author or founder. You can also highlight a person who has been positively impacted and is willing to share his or her experience. Having the WHO be someone whose life was changed forever by the WHAT is always best.

WHEN – You always want to clarify if your announcement is related to a timely event, campaign or contest. It is important to answer the question "Why Now?" to create a sense of urgency. If you write a social media post that says TOMORROW, your readers will definitely pay more attention. If you can associate your announcement with a current event, breaking news, holiday, or season, it will give your content even more traction with the media.

WHERE – When you pitch, you also want to include the WHERE. It could be your spokesperson's city, business address and/or the location for an event. You want to be really specific with reporters and the public so they can easily support whatever you are doing. The WHERE can also be a website page with a Call to Action such as buy the book on *Amazon*, enter a contest on *Facebook*, RSVP for an event through *Eventbrite*, sign up for a program, or vote on a website.

WHY – No matter what type of content you are sharing, you always want to be thinking "Why should anyone care?" and "How can this story help others?" If you post content that is "all about you," your audience will walk away in a split second. Alternatively, if you can clearly explain why this announcement impacts the reader and/or helps others have a better life, people will definitely pay more attention to your posts.

When writing a press release or pitch, you always want to ask "Why would the media want to cover this topic?" You never want to sound like an advertisement when approaching reporters. Instead, you want to present meaningful content, along with a personal impact story that connects to your audience.

■ Important Note: PR Content Is Not Sales Copy

It is very important to note that if your content objective is hardcore sales of books or products, it will not work for PR. Sales copy is a separate art from writing compelling content with unlimited strength to engage fans and get booked for media interviews. Great content should always educate and entertain versus oversell. With powerful content, you can brand a company or an expert as the go-to source to solve a problem. As a result, sales will come more naturally by building your credibility. If you want direct sales copy for your website, hire a copywriting expert with that skillset for the best results.

For all of your content, speak from the heart to your core audience to make your message stand the test of time.

■ *Goody PR* Case Study Example: *Warriors Heart Foundation* Awareness Campaign and Flag Art Fundraiser

We recently worked on a *Warriors Heart Foundation* Awareness Campaign and Flag Art Fundraiser with one of their Honorary Board of Advisors Members with an incredibly inspiring story. If you read the stories online, you would never know that it took several calls over three days to define the campaign in a clear, concise, and compelling way.

As background, *U.S. Air Force* Colonel (Ret.) Chris Stricklin purchased two wooden American flags made by veterans and first responders in the *Warriors Heart* Wood and Metal Shop during residential treatment for addiction and PTSD. Stricklin was planning a raffle and silent auction for these handmade American flags and wanted to draw as much publicity to *Warriors Heart* as possible.

Because Flag Day (June 14) was about ten days away, I recommended connecting the campaign launch to this holiday and continuing through July 4 (America's birthday). We also decided the best approach was to position these unique flags as "art pieces" versus something you would buy from an assembly line. We decided to emphasize that the flags were hand-signed by the warrior who made them.

When the campaign came together in one paragraph, it was very compelling and resulted in three powerful TV interviews in three weeks.

Here is the press release summary, plus a breakdown of the five Ws:

Press Release Headline and Opening Paragraph:

HEADLINE

U.S. Air Force Col (Ret.) Launches *Warriors Heart Foundation* Awareness Campaign on Flag Day

BODY

U.S. Air Force Colonel (Ret.) Chris R. Stricklin announces a *Warriors Heart Foundation* Awareness Campaign and Fundraiser from Flag Day (June 14) to Liberty Day (June 30). Anyone can support this effort and win one of two handcrafted flags by *Warriors Heart* clients through Stricklin's Protecting Our Protectors *Facebook* event and donation pages. All proceeds from this flag artwork raffle and silent auction will help provide residential treatment for warriors (military, veterans, and first responders) overcoming their War at Home with chemical dependencies, PTSD (Post-Traumatic Stress Disorder), mild TBI (Traumatic Brain Injury), and other recurring symptoms.

The five Ws are all in this first paragraph to make it really easy for anyone reading it. Let's take a closer look.

> **■ Five Ws Case Study Example: *Warriors Heart Foundation* Awareness Campaign and Fundraiser**
>
> - WHAT – *Warriors Heart Foundation* Awareness Campaign and Fundraiser
> - WHO – The spokesperson was *U.S. Air Force* Colonel (Ret.) Chris R. Stricklin, who is a member of *Warriors Heart Foundation* Honorary Board of Advisors and served 23 years in *U.S. Air Force*.
> - WHY – All proceeds from this flag artwork raffle and silent auction will help provide residential treatment for warriors struggling with chemical dependencies, PTSD (Post-Traumatic Stress Disorder), mild TBI (Traumatic Brain Injury), and other recurring symptoms.
> - WHEN – The raffle ran from Flag Day (June 14) to Liberty Day (June 30) 2018. The campaign was extended to July 4 to cover stories about the results and winners.
> - WHERE – Anyone can enter the raffle and silent auction for two flags handmade by *Warriors Heart* clients on Stricklin's Protecting Our Protectors *Facebook* fundraiser page.

Our main challenge for this campaign was juggling six potential URLs because of everyone involved. The URLs included WarriorsHeart.com, *Warriors Heart Facebook*, WarriorsHeartFoundation.org, Operation *Warriors Heart Foundation Facebook*, and two *Facebook* pages created by Stricklin highlighting the fundraiser and Liberty Day Festival and Parade event. The winners were to be selected at the Liberty Day Festival in Stricklin's hometown outside Birmingham, Alabama.

Even though the WarriorsHeartFoundation.org URL was featured in our media pitch as the main website, WarriorsHeart.com was referenced by all three TV stations as the place to get more information. Because the foundation was also on top of WarriorsHeart.com, this URL worked fine as the primary website. However, it's important to emphasize that the media is always looking for the easiest approach. They selected the shortest URL in the pitches.

We will talk more about this PR campaign's success later and the three very different TV interviews on *NBC Bay Area*, *CBS 46 Atlanta*, and *CBS 42 Birmingham* news stations. As a result of a team effort, Stricklin's campaign and fundraiser resulted in over $10,000 in donations to *Warriors Heart Foundation*.

Step 3.2 Write a Compelling Headline with Eight Words or Less

If you are writing a press release, media pitch, or even a *YouTube* video title, the headline can mean the difference between the reader paying attention or completely ignoring your content. Focus on writing headlines that are an announcement with a verb, and emphasize "how the brand is helping others."

No one wants to be around people who only care about sharing their story. These megaphone hogs are a boring turn-off to all audiences (media, fans, and family). Avoid turning readers away, and instead, find ways to engage in two-way conversations by adding meaning—in eight words or less—to your titles.

It is also important to write a title that is unique rather than what everyone else is saying about the same story. Remember our *Hunger Games* Cast video? The "Jennifer Lawrence Kisses at *Comic-Con*" in the headline was a major part of the magic!

CASE STUDY EXAMPLES – 2018 ROYAL WEDDING HEADLINES

Let's take a closer look at headline news examples found online for the royal wedding of Prince Harry to American actress and now Duchess of Sussex Meghan Markle. Take a close look to see how different reporters tried to grab your attention.

Keep in mind that when you pitch a reporter, they look at your email subject line as a potential headline. You can't underestimate the importance of titles. Be honest, which one of these story headlines makes you want to read it first?

ORIGINAL — 2018 Royal Wedding Headlines: "How Harry and Meghan Met"	
Headline 1 (8 words)	Royal wedding 2018: Prince Harry, Meghan Markle marry
Headline 2 (9 words)	Inside Meghan Markle and Prince Harry's Royal Wedding Receptions
Headline 3 (9 words)	Prince Harry and Meghan Markle marry in trailblazing ceremony
Headline 4 (14 words)	Prince Harry Gave Meghan Markle the Sweetest Look When their Wedding Reading Mentioned Children
Headline 5 (11 words)	Meghan Markle Reportedly Helped Heal Prince Harry's Relationship with Prince Charles
Headline 6 (15 words)	Meghan Markle: Prince Harry wife 'made it clear' he should bond with 'kind' Prince Charles
Headline 7 (11 words)	The Truth About the Royal Wedding Rumors That Everyone's Talking About
Headline 8 (11 words)	Bad breath, Serena's shoes, and Henry who? Your royal wedding debrief

Some of these story headlines are more compelling than others. Headlines 4, 5, and 7 are my favorites from this original list. However, the ones that are most compelling are too long. Here is how we would revise some of these headlines into eight words or less and still have attention grabbers.

REVISED 2018 Royal Wedding Headlines – 8 Words or Less	
Headline 2 (8 words)	Inside Meghan Markle and Prince Harry's Royal Receptions
Headline 4 (8 words)	Prince Harry Gave Meghan Markle the Sweetest Look
Headline 5 (8 words)	Markle Reportedly Helped Prince Harry's Father-Son Relationship
Headline 6 (8 words)	Meghan Markle: Prince Harry wife 'made it clear'
Headline 7 (7 words)	The Truth About the Royal Wedding Rumors

REVISED 2018 Royal Wedding Headlines - 8 Words or Less	
Headline 8 (8 words)	Royal Wedding bad breath, Serena's shoes, and Henry?

By removing the excess words, you can still write a compelling headline that will entice your audience to read more. You do not really need to know when Harry gave Meghan the "Sweetest Look." The words "Sweetest Look" trigger enough emotion to make you want to click on this story, regardless of when it happened.

It is also always best to have an action verb in story headlines, press releases, video titles and pitches. For example, the best royal wedding headlines include a verb:

VERBS in Revised Headlines — 2018 Royal Wedding Headlines	
Headline 4 (8 words)	Prince Harry <u>Gave</u> Meghan Markle the Sweetest Look
Headline 5 (8 words)	Markle Reportedly <u>Helped</u> Prince Harry's Father-Son Relationship
Headline 6 (8 words)	Meghan Markle: Prince Harry wife '<u>made</u> it clear'

Our favorite royal wedding headline by far would be this revision:

FAVORITE — 2018 Royal Wedding Headlines	
Headline 4 (8 words)	Prince Harry Gave Meghan Markle the Sweetest Look

This Royal Wedding headline is clear, concise, and compelling with emotion. Everyone watching any wedding is always looking for those magic moments of true love. This title should tempt the majority of your audience to take a closer look at the story because you can expect a visual image of the happy couple with the "sweetest look."

The bottom line is that you need to get the reader or potential customer to click on your content or you will get nowhere with your awareness, sales, fans, influencer support, engagements, and/or media interviews.

As you know, we live in an information age where the majority of people are reading content on their smartphones. In the future, many will read news via smart glasses or other objects. When I met a reporter from the *New York Times* at *CES* (*Consumer Electronics Show*) in Las Vegas, Nevada, he explained that his sole job was to prepare the paper for the future of reader consumption and technology. We have already seen live TV images on the mirror in luxury hotels. Are we ready for these big changes?

No matter what type of technology people use to consume their news and content, it all starts with a compelling headline with unlimited strength to attract readers.

Step 3.3 Write a Clear and Concise One-Sentence Summary

Once someone clicks on your headline, your next challenge is to grab their attention in the first sentence. While this might sound easy, it is not. You must write a clear and concise opening with a reason to continue reading. To make this happen, be prepared to revise the first sentence ten times until it sounds compelling.

Let's look at the first sentence of each of these Royal Wedding stories to see which one has the strongest opening.

ACTUAL RESULTS — 2018 Royal Wedding Headlines: "How Harry and Meghan Met"		First Sentence
Headline 1 (8 words) *Washington Post*	Royal wedding 2018: Prince Harry, Meghan Markle marry	The procession!
Headline 2 (9 words) *The Cut*	Inside Meghan Markle and Prince Harry's Royal Wedding Receptions	Meghan Markle and Prince Harry were (finally) married in a very royal wedding ceremony on Saturday, which was attended by 600 invited guests, a ton of members of the public, and, oh, just an estimated 1.9 billion people watching worldwide.

ACTUAL RESULTS — 2018 Royal Wedding Headlines: "How Harry and Meghan Met"		First Sentence
Headline 3 (9 words) CNN	Prince Harry and Meghan Markle marry in trailblazing ceremony	Britain's Prince Harry and American actress Meghan Markle sealed their wedding vows with a kiss on the steps outside St. George's Chapel in Windsor on Saturday, after a groundbreaking ceremony that didn't challenge royal norms so much as drive a gilded coach and horses through them.
Headline 4 (14 words) Town and Country Magazine	Prince Harry Gave Meghan Markle the Sweetest Look When their Wedding Reading Mentioned Children	The royal wedding was full of knowing glances and sweet moments of PDA between the bride and groom.
Headline 5 (11 words) Harper's Bazaar	Meghan Markle Reportedly Helped Heal Prince Harry's Relationship with Prince Charles	Falling for Meghan Markle not only gave Prince Harry a life partner, it also supposedly led to a better relationship with his dad, Prince Charles.
Headline 6 (15 words) Roll Daily	Meghan Markle: Prince Harry wife 'made it clear' he should bond with 'kind' Prince Charles	MEGHAN MARKLE is the wife of Prince Harry and the daughter-in-law of Prince Charles, following a royal wedding ceremony earlier this month on May 19.
Headline 7 (11 words) Town and Country Magazine	The Truth About the Royal Wedding Rumors That Everyone's Talking About	The months before the royal wedding were rife with speculation, from who would design the dress to the reception menu to potential gifts.
Headline 8 (11 words) The Guardian	Bad breath, Serena's shoes, and Henry who? Your royal wedding debrief	It's almost a British tradition: waking up on the Monday after a frantic wedding weekend, once the fog of Sunday's hangover has cleared, you can finally face looking back through social media feeds to see if your hazy recollections can really be true.

If you read through the first paragraph, our favorites continue to be stories 4, 5, and 7. And Headline 4 is still the best because the opening makes me want to fall in love all over again. The words describing their body language and adoration for each other are very powerful. Everyone with a heart will want to continue reading this story to see photographs of the royal couple's PDA moments.

FAVORITE OPENING — Royal Wedding 2018 Headlines: "How Harry and Meghan Met"		First Sentence
Headline 4 (14 words) *Town and Country Magazine*	Prince Harry Gave Meghan Markle the Sweetest Look When their Wedding Reading Mentioned Children	The royal wedding was full of knowing glances and sweet moments of PDA between the bride and groom.

In comparison, it is interesting to look at two different angles on the same topic in stories 5 and 6:

SAME TOPIC COMPARISON — 2018 Royal Wedding Headlines: "How Harry and Meghan Met"		First Sentence
Headline 5 (11 words) *Harper's Bazaar*	Meghan Markle Reportedly Helped Heal Prince Harry's Relationship with Prince Charles	Falling for Meghan Markle not only gave Prince Harry a life partner, it also supposedly led to a better relationship with his dad, Prince Charles.
Headline 6 (15 words) *Roll Daily*	Meghan Markle: Prince Harry wife 'made it clear' he should bond with 'kind' Prince Charles	MEGHAN MARKLE is the wife of Prince Harry and the daughter-in-law of Prince Charles, following a royal wedding ceremony earlier this month on May 19.

Without a doubt, the first sentence is ten times stronger in the Headline 5 story. This opening gets right to the point about what they are going to cover and creates an emotional response that makes you want to read more. The first paragraph for the Headline 6 story is much more of an "announcement" statement and does not connect with the headline.

Step 3.4 Add a Quote from the Heart to Emphasize Your Message

It is also helpful to add a quote from the heart to a story, press release, media pitch or website content for emphasis and meaning. Let's look at some of the moving quotes we found in these royal wedding stories:

QUOTES — 2018 Royal Wedding Headlines: "How Harry and Meghan Met"		Compelling Quote
Headline 4 (14 words) *Town and Country Magazine*	Prince Harry Gave Meghan Markle the Sweetest Look When their Wedding Reading Mentioned Children	The royal wedding service started with the Right Reverend David Conner reading the preface. The second he says, "[Marriage] is given as the foundation of family life in which children are born and nurtured and in which each member of the family, in good times and in bad, may find strength, companionship and comfort, and grow to maturity in love," Prince Harry turned to his bride with the biggest grin.
Headline 5 (11 words) *Harper's Bazaar*	Meghan Markle Reportedly Helped Heal Prince Harry's Relationship with Prince Charles	"Meghan met Charles and was bowled over by his charm," a "family source" told the Mail. "She told Harry he was wonderful: welcoming, warm, hard-working, kind and stable."
Headline 6 (15 words) *Roll Daily*	Meghan Markle: Prince Harry wife 'made it clear' he should bond with 'kind' Prince Charles	"Meghan met Charles and was bowled over by his charm," said a source.

In our opinion, the Headline 5 story quote is the most moving. In Headline 4, the reporter is directly quoting a reading, and it is really long. This reading quote could be cut in half and still get the same result. The Headline 6 quote is a little too short to move mountains of emotions.

Liz H. Kelly

As a summary, let's switch over to less exciting topics (royal weddings are pretty darn compelling). Check out these headlines, openings, and quotes for *Goody PR* press releases for different industries. You can really turn almost any announcement into a compelling story with the right headline and authentic quotes, and yes, these are far from perfect. We could re-write these releases for hours!

Case Study Examples — *Goody PR* Press Releases		
Headline	**First Sentence**	**Compelling Quote**
Goody Awards to honor *Free2Luv* Co-Founder Tonya Sandis at Unstoppable Empowerment Event (12 words)	*Free2Luv* Co-Founder Tonya Sandis will be presented with a *Golden Goody Award* (top humanitarian award presented by the *Goody Awards*) at their benefit fundraiser UNSTOPPABLE Empowerment Event this Saturday, March 10, 2018, at *The Regent DTLA*, 12:00-3:30pm, in Los Angeles, California.	"We love everything *Free2Luv* does to promote the self-esteem for youth and are grateful to Tonya's fans for nominating her for our top award." ~ Liz H Kelly, *Goody Awards* Founder
Robert Kiyosaki and *Rich Dad Advisors* to Release New Book 'More Important Than Money' (14 words)	To emphasize business is a team sport, Best-Selling Author Robert Kiyosaki ("Rich Dad Poor Dad") and his eight *Rich Dad Advisors* will release a new book, "More Important Than Money, An Entrepreneur's Team" (May 30, 2017) at *Book Expo America* (BEA) on June 1-2, 2017, in New York City.	In this new book, Robert Kiyosaki emphasizes, "Many people have million-dollar ideas. They're confident that their new product or service or innovation will make them rich and that all their dreams will come true. The problem is: Most people don't know how to turn their million-dollar idea into millions of dollars."

Case Study Examples — *Goody PR* Press Releases		
Headline	First Sentence	Compelling Quote
Top 1 Percent Realtor Debbi DiMaggio Releases 7 Real Estate Success Tips (12 words)	As the spring real estate buying season hits a peak, author, Realtor, parent, and speaker Debbi DiMaggio releases her Top 7 Tips for "How to Elevate Yourself into the Top 1 Percent" in a new book, "The Art of Real Estate" co-authored with husband/partner Adam Betta.	"The biggest piece of advice I can share is to stop making excuses, take advice, follow it and get moving." - Debbi DiMaggio, Top 1 Percent Realtor

While we did not get these headlines to fit into eight words, the keywords are in the beginning. Always place the most important words in the front of a title because that is what people will see in *Google* search results. The quotes made these announcements even more real and explained the background and benefits.

Step 3.5 Tell a Compelling Story in 300 to 800 Words

Now that we have reviewed story headlines, press release titles, first sentences, and compelling quotes, let's look at how to put it all together. Telling a story in 300 to 800 words is the best length, but is not easy. We often work five to ten hours on a one-page press release or story to make it clear and a strong representation of the brand. It has to immediately answer the five Ws (What, Who, Where, When and Why) with meaning to capture the audience's attention.

Goody PR always sends a draft to the client for review and emphasizes that short is better. Inevitably, many clients expand an 800-word draft into a 1,200-word press release or column because they know too much information. Because the majority of people do not want to read long stories, we work with them on multiple versions until the content is moving and under 800 words. The final version is always a negotiation of words.

8-SECOND PR WORD ARTIST

To magnify your brand, the best thing to do is think of yourself as a "Word Artist." We can't emphasize enough the importance of getting to the point immediately in the age of short attention spans. Words mean everything in your PR, marketing and social media marketing.

When you write your first version of anything, recognize that it is a very rough draft. After you revise it several times, your story can have long-term durability. Sure, you can write it faster, but it will not be nearly as powerful.

One of my favorite classes EVER was a Business Writing class at the *University of Maryland*, College Park. The professor told us on the first day, "When you turn in your papers, you will automatically get a C. If you implement my feedback and turn it back in, you can earn a B. And if you take the feedback on the second version, and write a third version, you may get an A."

This professor changed my life and career significantly. While most people do not have the patience to write several drafts, it really makes a huge difference in the marketing profession. When you are writing content, it is so important to read it out loud to see if it makes sense. Then, test the message on others. This editing process will help you fine-tune your content, reach more people, and increase sales. Invest time in your content because it speaks volumes for your brand.

The easiest way to start writing anything (book, blog, press release) is with an outline. Within an outline, your key points can become subtitles, chapters, bulleted lists, quotes, statistics, and case studies to keep the reader engaged. To avoid writer's block, start anything with a list of topics and then fill in the details.

Once the big picture is clear, the story can then provide a roadmap. To answer the question, why should anyone care, always provide helpful tips for your audience. This information may include a top ten list, key resources, and/or a new product or service to enhance their lives or business.

For example, our client Tom the Tax Expert launched a new three-day CPA class. To find out what should be in the press release, Tom advised us to "listen to my podcast" to find out what will be covered. While this approach was not the most efficient way to get the story, I listened to the podcast twice. Afterwards, the content was turned into a short, concise, and clear message using easy-to-read bullet points.

For PR professionals, many clients do not know what they know. Your job is to find and magnify the message. In this case, Tom knew what he wanted to cover in this class. However, he did not know how to convey it to us quickly.

The story became clear when Tom said, "We are going to talk about education, team, systems, and mission." This one line in his podcast was the content gold. Let's take a closer look at how this all came together for the press release.

■ Case Study Example – From Podcast to Press Release

Press Release HEADLINE: CPA Tom Wheelwright Launches *Tax-Free Wealth Network* with 3-Day CPA Event

SUMMARY: All CPAs are invited to this free *Tax-Free Wealth Network* (TFWN) inaugural education program "The CPA-Revolution Masterclass." The program will cover four success pillars for building a more profitable CPA practice:

4 SUCCESS PILLARS:
- Pillar 1 – Training and Education – This event will cover how better education and experience can lead to a higher level of "confidence" in the CPA and clients.
- Pillar 2 – Team – This program will cover the power of team for CPAs, and Wheelwright's secrets for how he's built profitable businesses through partners, employees, and contractors with complementary areas of expertise.
- Pillar 3 – Systems and Procedures – Wheelwright will expand on why systems have been the "secret sauce" for building successful CPA businesses guaranteed to reduce client taxes by 10 to 40 percent.
- Pillar 4 – Mission and Identity – Examples for how to brand a CPA business will be reviewed with best practices from Wheelwright.

The entire press release ended up being 776 words (just under the 800-word best practice guideline for press releases) and was picked up online by 213 media outlets (*The Boston Globe, Los Angeles Business Journal, Markets Insider*, and many local TV stations). To get this type of response, a release needs to be written in an easy-to-read format with helpful content. Of course, there are other important factors to consider in terms of the newswire service, keywords, and links. However, the most important factor in a press release's success is the content.

Step 3.6 Include Credible References and Statistics

Two other elements that can add a lot of value to a story on any platform are references with verifiable statistics. You can increase your content's credibility instantly by including numbers with credible sources. These numbers help explain the problem that you are trying to solve, and make a story pitch more relevant to a reporter.

We have spent hours searching for the health trend statistics to support *Warriors Heart* residential treatment program press releases. Statistics have included addiction rates for drugs and alcohol, opioid epidemic numbers, mental health studies, and suicide rates for warriors.

When you search online, you always want to find the most current and solid reference, and include the exact website URL in press releases, pitches and blogs. Here are three examples of our research findings on the unacceptable veteran suicide rate in the U.S. that *Warriors Heart* works so hard to prevent:

■ Research Statistics to Support Content - Veteran Suicide Rate Example

Search Result 1 - Best:

Today the U.S. Department of Veterans Affairs (VA) released findings from its most recent analysis of Veteran suicide data for all 50 states and the District of Columbia....The average number of Veterans who died by suicide each day remained unchanged at 20.

Source: *Veterans Administration* Press Release (July 2018)

Search Result 2 – Older data that shows a small change:

Compared to the data from the 2012 report, which estimated the number of Veteran deaths by suicide to be 22 per day, the current analysis indicates that in 2014 an average of 20 Veterans a day died from suicide.

Source: *Veterans Administration (August 2016)*
VA Releases Report on Nation's Largest Analysis of Veteran Suicide

---

Search Result 3 – Older data with solid CDC reference:

The new study includes more than 50 million veterans' records from 1979 to 2014, including every state. The data, compiled over the last four years, also comes from the Centers for Disease Control.

Source: *Military Times (July 2016)*
New VA Study finds 20 Veterans Commit Suicide Each Day

It is so important to get these numbers right. And if you are pitching a reporter, he or she will be grateful because you made their job easier. Of course, they may check another source, but the fact that you sent the numbers with references will help you build long-term relationships with producers and writers.

Your readers and reporters will also come back for more if they know you take time to make sure your information is accurate.

Step 3.7 Choose the Best Press Release Distribution System

Once your story is written with optimal strength, including the headline, opening, and five Ws, your next step is finding the right distribution platform. While many people post a news announcement as a blog on their website and/or email it to reporters, a press release distribution system can make your message travel much farther and faster.

The cost and methods for sending out a press release vary greatly. Many PR professionals now question whether sending out a press release is even valuable. It is extremely rare today to get a call from a reporter in response to a press release. In every case, you still need to pitch individual reporters with your release with a powerful media hook for the best earned media results.

One of the biggest benefits of a press release is the SEO. As long as you write high-quality content and use a good distribution platform, the release will get picked up online by multiple outlets and show up in *Google* search results for years.

You can post a press release easily on a free service website. However, you really get what you pay for with press releases. Free releases will go nowhere and simply be a page online. Sure, you can email the link to reporters. However, if someone is searching for your specific topic online, they will never find it.

When working with *Goody PR* clients, we have used these three different press release services for various reasons. Here's a quick recap of options for you as a guide:

Press Release Distribution Service	Key Benefits	Limitations	2018 Costs
PR Web*	Lower cost, good distribution, 24/7 customer service	No word limit. No limits on adding images. Additional services available for a fee.	$389 for a national release with a video. Release is delivered directly to targeted media list by topic. Release includes a comprehensive report.
Business Wire*	Middle-of-the-road costs, you can go national or target delivery to a specific geographic area	400-word limit. Includes one logo image. Additional charges may apply.	Approximately $600 for a 400-word regional release. Release is delivered directly to targeted media lists. Additional charges for extra words, images, and social media report.
PR Newswire*	High-end release	400-word limit. Additional charges may apply and are the most costly.	Approximately $800 for a national release with 400 words. Release is delivered directly to targeted media list. Additional charges for extra words. PLUS $350 for any images. Release includes comprehensive report.

*NOTE: All press release prices and packaging are subject to change. You should contact the company for their fee structure.

While we have spent many hours talking to all three press release services, we usually send out announcements via *PR Web* because the primary goal is SEO. Many of our clients have sent out monthly releases for years as an overall SEO strategy.

Alternatively, we used *Business Wire* for a client in Canada who wanted a hyper-local focus for their release. In this case, the release went to media in their province only.

For major news announcements, *Goody PR* clients have used *PR Newswire*. The costs have ranged from $921 to $1,890. This high-end cost is off-the-charts because the client did not want to cut words. While *PR Newswire* is considered the best by far, it requires the biggest budget. It's probably worth the investment for a major launch announcement, but you don't need this top-of-the-line service for monthly releases.

It's also important to keep in mind that the best days to send out press releases are Tuesdays, Wednesdays and Thursdays. Most reporters are overwhelmed on Mondays, and are wrapping up stories on Fridays for the week.

Each press release distribution service will send you a detailed summary report, and the majority of the online pickups and engagements happen in the first 24 to 48 hours. The numbers may change within the first thirty days, but the initial response is really the most important.

You can also send a pre-release notice out to a specific group of reporters before the content is sent out via a news wire. Some reporters prefer to break the story first, and advance notice gives them this opportunity.

Another option is to send out a pre-release to specific reporters one at a time and ask if they would like to have an "exclusive" interview. This exclusive story pitch email should include a deadline for a yes or no answer, and is usually offered only to major media competing for the same story.

Step 3.8 Proofread. Test. Proofread.

Your final step in creating compelling content with the unlimited strength is to proofread, test, and proofread again. Here are some steps you can take during this review process:

■ *8-Second PR* Proofreading Process

1. Use Spellcheck – Yes, spellcheck should be an obvious step, but many of my *UCLA Extension* digital marketing students do not use it, and it drives me bonkers! It only takes a few minutes to use it, so just do it! Spellcheck will not catch everything such as missing words or the wrong version of a word, but it is a good start.

2. Read It Out Loud – It can help to read your content out loud before sharing it to see if the story flows and is conversational.

3. Send It to a Friend with No Background Information – You can also send your draft to a friend without explaining the content. Ask them to read it and provide honest feedback. If they are moved and cannot find typos, you know your content is good to go.

4. Email Draft to Yourself – You can also email a draft to yourself and then read it on your phone away from your office. I email every pitch to myself as part of the quality review process, and it makes a huge difference. If a pitch email is clear on your mobile phone, then it's ready to send out. (P.S. The majority of reporters open emails on their smartphone so keep it short!)

5. Send It to Your Client – After you complete steps one through four, send the draft to your client (if appropriate) and ask for their feedback and edits. *Goody PR* sends press release and column drafts to clients for review. However, we do not share pitches for a variety of reasons.

6. Use Track Changes – When reviewing documents with other parties, always ask them to use Track Changes so you can see exactly what they changed. You can also use *Google docs* or *Dropbox* to exchange files and track edits.

7. Use Version Control – Version control management of documents is very important to save time and preserve accuracy. We give documents a version number (example v1) plus the date in the file name. If you are using something like *Google docs*, it will usually track the last person who made edits and timestamp it.

8. Repeat Proofreading Process – Once you receive edits or make changes, go back to Step 1 and repeat this *8-Second PR* Proofreading Cycle. You do not want to accept changes automatically. Always go through the content again carefully.

Once your content is triple-checked on multiple devices, then it's time to publish and share your story with the world! It is best to not make changes after it is published. However, we all make mistakes. If there are any typos or incorrect facts, it is important to update the content ASAP.

CHAPTER 3 RECAP

Are you ready now to write compelling content with the unstoppable strength to captivate both fans and reporters? With the new tools in this chapter for writing headlines, press releases, blogs, quotes, first paragraphs, media pitches and solid statistics, you have what you need. Yes, you can write content that demands the same attention and durability of a superhero.

Here is a recap of the action items we have covered, your new Unlimited Content Strength PR Superpower, and challenges.

Step 3 Action Items — Write Compelling Content with Unlimited Strength to Move Readers

1. Define what you are announcing to the world.

2. Write a compelling headline with eight words or less.

3. Write a clear and concise one-sentence summary.

4. Add a quote from the heart to emphasize your message.

5. Tell a compelling story in 300 to 800 words.

6. Include credible references and statistics.

7. Choose the best press release distribution system.

8. Proofread. Test. Proofread.

PR Superpower 3 — Unlimited Content Strength PR Superpower

With the average adult attention span being shorter than ever before, getting to the point in a compelling way is one of the most important skills for all marketing professionals. You cannot afford to take chances with sloppy or lengthy content that has no connection with the reader.

To get new ideas for content, *Google* your topic, then click "News" to see what headlines already exist. For your pitch, blog or video, choose a different eight-ten word title with a verb to peak more interest.

Your Unlimited Content Strength PR Superpower can help you get the undivided attention of readers. All of these superhero strengths can add to your enhanced marketing skills for Immediate and Ultimate Media Success!

Chapter 3 — 8-Second PR Challenges

As we close Chapter 3, here are your *8-Second PR* Challenges:

1. What are five compelling announcements and headlines you can write in eight words or less about your brand, product, or service?
2. What are 3 evergreen stories that you can pitch?
3. How will the first sentence for each piece of content compel the reader to continue?
4. Whom can you quote to add value to the content?
5. What statistics can add strength to your story?
6. What is the high-level outline for your content?
7. Are you going to send out press releases, and which service will you use?
8. Who is going to proofread your content and/or provide feedback?

You can now give any story more energy with your new *8-Second* PR Superpowers. You know how to be a Word Artist, so just start writing your first draft. With these advanced content writing skills, you can connect with your audience and reporters at warp speed. Remember, you are going to write at least three versions, so the sooner you get started, the faster you can release your message and get earned media.

In the next chapter, we will take a closer look at writing a compelling hook to get the media even more interested in covering your personal or business brand. Are you having fun now with this creative storytelling process? Let's keep moving forward by building upon your story.

STEP 4

Write Powerful Media Hooks to Connect with Reporters

"Your PR clients do not realize what they know. Ask a lot of questions so you can help them present their story."

—CHUCK MCCULLOUGH, SAN ANTONIO EXPRESS-NEWS AND
FREELANCE REPORTER FOR 30+ YEARS OF EXPERIENCE

D o you have ten media hooks with a moving story that you can pitch reporters? While you can always write a great column or press release, remember it is much more valuable to get reporters to cover your story as earned media versus paid media. When you pitch the media, the story "hook" is what immediately grabs their attention, or not.

It is not enough to say, "write a story about my cool company"; there needs to be a powerful WHY and WHY NOW. You always want to explain how you are helping others. Most clients will say, "We want people to know about what we do." Well, that media hook will never stick without a powerful backstory.

To get the media's attention, you must pitch a timely topic that can both entertain and educate their audience. In all cases, it is best to pitch how your company, product, book, or service is improving lives. You also need to explain why the story is relevant today. If you have a "spokesperson" who is willing to share their personal story about how you helped them, that will significantly increase your chances of coverage.

■ **PR Superpower 4 – Media Hook Superpower**

To help your brand get more earned media (where someone else shares your story through TV, radio, print or digital), use the **Media Hook Superpower**. You always want to pitch a powerful media hook to make your ideas resonate with the reporter. With an eight-second adult attention span, you need to immediately grab the reporter's interest in your email subject line, pitch headline and/or first sentence. Once you have sold the right reporter on your story idea, their media coverage can give your brand way more credibility than any paid advertisement. If you build a good relationship with the reporter and have a reputation that you are "easy to work with and provide great content," they will keep coming back for more. Use these story pitching tips and *8-Second PR* Superpower to make lasting impressions, and extend your long-term Ultimate Media Success!

If a reporter is not immediately sold on your story idea, you can always go back and try again later with a different hook for the same client. Pitching the media is a delicate dance where you have to learn when to push and when to back off.

Let's go through how you can improve your chances of media coverage.

STEP 4 ACTION ITEMS — WRITE POWERFUL MEDIA HOOKS TO CONNECT WITH REPORTERS

1. Write an eight-word email subject with a moving story hook.
2. Define a clear and compelling hook in the first sentence of every pitch.
3. Define the star(s) in each story pitch.
4. Define why the story is relevant and timely.
5. Define HOW you are helping others improve their lives.
6. Define three to eight talking points to support your story hook.
7. Provide supporting media for your story pitch.
8. Test Media Hooks A, B, C and repeat.

PR SUPERPOWER 4 — MEDIA HOOK SUPERPOWER

Consider your story options and pitch the right media hook to the right outlet and reporters at the right time. For example, TV is very visual and tends to be short interviews. Radio interviews tend to be longer with niche audiences. Print interviews can be much more involved or be a quote or mention in a bigger story with multiple experts.

If a pitch is customized for a specific media outlet, it will always get the best response. For example, you should pitch different interview topics to *TMZ Live* versus *CNN* about the same book (more on this later).

STEP 4.1 WRITE AN EIGHT-WORD EMAIL SUBJECT WITH A MOVING MEDIA HOOK

When you email a pitch to a reporter, the subject line plays a critical role in determining whether they will open it or not. Writing a catchy subject line is a must. There is a reason that people hire PR and email marketing pros to get more eyeballs on their story. In this chapter, you will learn some of our secrets with examples.

To make your story more "newsworthy," your best bet is to tie the subject line to current headlines or timely events. For example, Thanksgiving is a very popular topic with lots of stories written about this U.S. holiday on the fourth Thursday of November.

Let's say you do PR for a real estate company in Boston, Massachusetts, that wants to do a Thanksgiving campaign to give back to their local community.

While interviewing the founder, whom we will call "Paul" in this book, you discover that he used to be homeless. This fact creates a powerful WHY and backstory for why Paul would want to help others in this situation. While brainstorming with Paul and his team, they decide to sponsor a "Rebuild Lives for Homeless This Holiday" Awareness Campaign and Fundraiser for the local shelter from November 1 through January 15.

Paul's awareness campaign will include a fundraiser for $50,000 to cover the costs of new beds, clothes, job skills training, and interview coaching to help homeless individuals get a job and rebuild their lives.

To find creative ways to present your media hook, you can *Google* "Thanksgiving" to see what is already out there. Reporters are always looking for a unique story so it's important to stand out.

For example, if you *Google* "Thanksgiving", a broad list of the latest media coverage will appear when you click the "News" tab. You can also narrow your search by adding the geography (city, country, region) and topics. Because Paul lives in Boston, try a searching "Thanksgiving" and "Boston" and "homeless". As a result, you will find what the media is covering already related to your topic:

GOOGLE RESULTS – THANKSGIVING NEWS: "Thanksgiving" and "Boston" and "homeless"	
News Story Headline	Media Hook Insights
Gas company offers thousands left homeless by Boston suburb explosions a free Thanksgiving dinner after mayor told corporation to 'get off their a**'	This is a great media hook because it is specific and helps others.
Flock to these turkey trots this Thanksgiving.	This is cute, but more of a tease.
Target to get an earlier start this Thanksgiving.	This is a retailer announcement, and is not very compelling compared to a personal story.
Ed Goldman: "Gobble Gobble Give" Is no gobbledygoop: Volunteers feed Sacramento hungry on Thanksgiving.	This is a great media hook because it has a fun campaign name, spokesperson and has impact.
John 3:16 Mission: *The Salvation Army* seek more donations for Thanksgiving	This headline is more of a call to action versus a media hook.
Campus ministers respond to hungry, homeless college students	This headline could be a good media hook. It depends on the backstory.

The good news is that it does not appear that anyone else has the same story as Paul.

For Paul's "Rebuild Lives for Homeless This Holiday" Campaign, there are multiple subject lines that you could use with different hooks. You sometimes have to call or pitch a reporter twenty times before they cover your story, so it is really important to get creative. Your email subject line and hook are one of the most important factors in getting on the media's radar.

As you become a stronger *8-Second PR* Word Artist, you will learn how to fine-tune your email subject lines to get a higher percentage of reporters reading your media hook. Asking a question (Who, What, and Why) is a great subject line strategy versus an event announcement.

In all cases, try a variety of subject line options to see what works best. You also want to test sending emails at different times of day. To learn from experience, use email software (*Constant Contact, Mailchimp*) that tells you the percent of reporters who actually opened your email, what time they read it and what links they clicked.

Let's look at some examples of potential email subject lines for Paul's Real Estate Company's campaign.

■ Email Subject Examples - Rebuild Lives for Homeless This Holiday

Subject 1 - Why Paul Is Rebuilding Lives for Homeless This Holiday

Subject 2 - Why X Co. Is Rebuilding Lives for Homeless This Holiday

Subject 3 - Why Former Homeless Founder Is Rebuilding Homeless Lives

Subject 3 - Why Boston CEO Is Rallying for the Homeless This Holiday

Subject 4 - Heartfelt Holiday Story - How New Homeless Program Will Rebuild Lives

Subject 5 - How New Homeless Program Will Provide Job Skills

Subject 6 - How Boston Can Rally for Homeless This Holiday

Subject 7 - Tomorrow - Boston Thanksgiving Campaign for Homeless Kicks Off

Subject 8 - How New Program Helps Homeless Get Jobs (and have examples)

Step 4.2 Define a Clear and Compelling Hook in the First Sentence of Every Pitch

Once you have attracted the right media to open your pitch email, the first sentence is by far the most important line. It's like any content, the first impression matters. If they do not understand what you are saying in the opening paragraph, you can forget about them covering your story.

You always want to think "Why would anyone care?" You also want to pitch differently to print, radio, and TV media. Writing different hooks based on the media format will get better results.

Print can cover more detail in longer stories. Radio is usually three minutes to one hour (usually a podcast is longer). TV likes props as visuals, and the length of most news segments ranges from 30 seconds to six minutes. Sadly, a social good story about a charity event tends to get the least amount of time on TV. A new book interview or news story with experts weighing is usually three to five minutes.

For Paul, the real estate company owner, you could pitch reporters who cover real estate, social good, business, and entrepreneurs. Depending on Paul's media experience and profile, you can pitch national and local TV, radio, and print outlets. If Paul has no experience on TV, it's best to pitch the local news before a national program.

Let's take a closer look at three examples of what we wrote in the first sentence of media pitches for *Goody PR* client Debbi DiMaggio that resulted in earned media for print, radio, and TV. As we've discussed previously, Debbi is a "Top 1 Percent Realtor," author, and philanthropist in the San Francisco Bay Area. She's written several books about real estate and has adopted five charities.

Publication	First Sentence in Email	Media Result
Unique Homes	As a potential real estate story on luxury home trends for *Unique Homes*, luxury home Realtor and author Debbi DiMaggio can discuss the latest trends that she will be sharing at the *Inman Luxury Connect* conference in Beverly Hills tomorrow.	National profile with feature story (one-page) that included a large photo of the author, book cover image, and great quotes.
KGO-AM	As a potential Consumer Talk with Michael Finney on *KGO-AM* story, San Francisco Realtors Debbi DiMaggio and Adam Betta can share business and real estate success tips based on their VIP Philosophy and DiMaggio charisma highlighted in their new book, *The Art of Real Estate*.	A 10-minute talk radio interview with Debbi DiMaggio and her husband/co-author on a top radio station in the San Francisco Bay Area.

Publication	First Sentence in Email	Media Result
ABC 7 Bay Area	(This email was sent after speaking to the newsroom.) I wanted to forward this pitch below for ABC 7's consideration for a Bay Area event tomorrow that is a Make-A-Wish type birthday party at *George Mark Children's House* in the East Bay hosted by philanthropist/Realtor Debbi DiMaggio, where the local police and fire departments are going to sing happy birthday to a brave young adult XXX between 12:30 and 1:30pm (address, CA) at her Love Bravely Birthday Party.	An inspiring social good TV story on *ABC 7* in San Francisco with Debbi speaking at the event, the young adult being honored blowing out the birthday candles, and the local fire and police singing happy birthday.

In this case, the *Unique Homes* story was a national piece, and the radio and TV were local news outlets. This coverage not only promoted the client's book, it helped build her personal and business brands as a luxury Realtor and philanthropist.

After this PR success, DiMaggio decided that she wanted to be part of a gifting suite in West Hollywood in celebration of the *Academy Awards*. Her goal was to set up an office in Los Angeles (along with San Francisco) with celebrity clients. For this event and media pitch, we took a very different approach with an entertainment spin.

By partnering with the event host, Doris Bergman, we came up with the media hook that Debbi was the "Realtor to the Stars." As background, Debbi is a cousin of baseball legend Joe DiMaggio, who was married to Marilyn Monroe.

In the story pitch, we highlighted her cousin and real estate client list that "reads like the credits of a Hollywood blockbuster, including celebrities such as Julianne Moore, Sally Field, Hugh Grant, Ted Danson, Tom Arnold, and Macaulay Culkin."

This celebration of Hollywood's biggest night also had a Valentine's Day theme. For the table display, we brainstormed ideas with DiMaggio. Her table had a black-and-white poster-size photo of Joe DiMaggio kissing Marilyn Monroe. Debbi gifted both celebrity guests and media chocolate truffles in *Tiffany Blue* boxes with red ribbons. Debbi also gave away her new book, *Lights, Camera, Action!* that compares buying a home with going on an audition as an actor. This fun book was illustrated by *DreamWorks* animator Steve Hickner, which was another entertainment spin.

This "Realtor to the Stars" media hook and event display were so successful that Debbi used this theme for four different gifting suites connected to awards season in Los Angeles. She received mentions in about forty earned media stories (around ten per event). After this PR strategy resulted in so much coverage and influencer awareness, DiMaggio achieved her goal to open a Beverly Hills office with a partner. (Debbi still has an office in San Francisco with her husband and travels back and forth.)

Step 4.3 Define the Star(s) in Each Story Pitch

A media story is rarely about a product. It's about how someone or something is positively changing lives. To illustrate this point, you want to be really clear about who is the star or spokesperson when pitching the media. If you are sending a story about a company, be clear about WHO specifically is available for an interview.

For the star of the story, you also want to provide a short biography that includes their personal connection and any media experience. To gain the interest of reporters, always provide the WHY behind the spokesperson.

If you ask someone for a short bio, it is often really hard for them to provide it in one paragraph. Your job is to find the gems and cut the bio down for the media to digest quickly. Being cute and clever is okay, but it is much more powerful to have concrete wins so the media can quickly determine if the person is a good media source.

Keep in mind that when a producer or reporter selects someone to interview, their reputation is on the line. They are always searching for a "sure bet" when booking experts on TV and radio.

For example, below is a comparison of two bios for the same person. We included this bio in media pitches for a new book launch. The author is pretty well-known with over 330,000 Twitter followers, but I recommended a more formal bio for book promotions.

■ Case Study Examples – Author and Expert Bios

Original Bio V1 from the book cover – DANNY ZUKER @ DannyZuker (AUTHOR) – When not delighting his hundreds of thousands of Twitter followers by trolling the leader of the free world, five-time Emmy Award winner DANNY ZUKER works as a television comedy writer/producer. He's spent the last nine years as an executive producer/writer on *Modern Family* and has worked on more than a dozen shows, including *Evening Shade, Roseanne, Just Shoot Me*, and, as Trump so cleverly tweeted at him, "so many flops."

Revised Bio V2 for the media – DANNY ZUKER @ DannyZuker is a five-time Emmy Award winner, comedy writer/producer, podcast host, TEDx Talk speaker, and AUTHOR of *He Started It!: My Twitter War with Trump (Sept 2018)*. Zuker is currently an executive producer/writer for ABC's hit comedy TV show *Modern Family*, where he's worked for the past nine years. Previously, Zuker worked on more than a dozen TV shows, including *Evening Shade, Roseanne, Just Shoot Me*, and, as Trump so cleverly tweeted at him, "so many flops." As a regular at the *Hollywood Improv* Comedy Club, Zuker is part of the Smash Story show team. Zuker started out as an intern on *The Howard Stern Show*. His work has appeared in many media, including *CNN, Good Day LA, KTLA, The Hollywood Reporter, Entertainment Weekly, Deadline, Mashable, The Hill, IFC, The Adam Carolla Show* and more. Zuker delights his hundreds of thousands of Twitter followers daily by trolling the leader of the free world.

Defining the spokesperson in story pitches is a must. If the pitch does not have a credible speaker and powerful backstory, it is going to be much harder to get coverage.

Step 4.4 Define Why the Story is Relevant and Timely

Making a story relevant and timely in your media hook can significantly increase the chances of a reporter or producer calling you for an interview. If you are writing a column, connecting it to headline news can also improve the likelihood that your story will be published by the editor.

If you do not answer the "Why Now" question, your story hook may take months to get media attention. This detail is important! Let's take a closer look at PR tips for ways to make your story relevant and timely.

RELEVANT MEDIA HOOK TIPS

The first thing you want to explain is how is the story hook relevant to the media outlet. The more specific you are in the pitch, the better.

Local News Connection – Was the spokesperson born in that city? Did they go to school there or teach school in that city? Are they hosting a local event there? Do they work in that city?

National News Connection – Is your "Who" or "What" tied to a national headline, trending topic, new study, bestseller book, blockbuster film, or more?

TIMELY MEDIA HOOK TIPS

Holiday Connections – Can your media hook be connected to a holiday (July 4, Thanksgiving, New Years, Memorial Day, Veterans Day)?

Seasonal Themes – Does your media hook have anything to do with different seasons such as fall fashion, winter blues, or New Year's resolutions?

Event Themes – Is there a major event happening that the media can cover? And how is this event helping the community?

NEWSJACK YOUR STORY PITCH

Newsjacking is the art of injecting your media hook into a news headline to generate coverage and social media engagement. This approach is one of the best ways to get your story picked up, which is why I constantly monitor breaking news.

Here are a few case-study examples of how this newsjacking worked so well:

> ### ■ *Goody PR* Newsjack Case Study 1 — Headline News – Book Comparison
>
> We were fortunate to have the *Chicago Tribune* write a review for Danny Zuker's new book, *He Started It!: My Twitter War with Trump* within 48 hours after launch because it was relevant to headline news. What made it so timely was *The Washington Post* reporter Bob Woodward's new book *Fear* was released about President Trump at the same time. Bob Woodward was being interviewed on major news channels and appearing in national newspaper headlines everywhere. During this book launch week, nationally syndicated political satirist and humor(ish) columnist Rex Huppke compared *He Started It!* to *Fear* by saying Zuker's book is "way shorter, way funnier and way easier to read."

You should always be looking for ways to connect your story to what everyone is already talking about on the news. Here is another very different example of how this approach works.

■ *Goody PR* Newsjack Case Study 2 — National Holiday – Memorial Day

When asked to do last minute PR for a Memorial Day movie premiere, the pitches resulted in two local TV interviews on major news stations in Los Angeles, including *KCBS* and *KTLA*.

The pitch email included a powerful media hook:
- WHO - 95-year-old WWII veteran Leon Cooper
- WHAT- New film premiere for "Return to the Philippines: The Leon Cooper Sequel" and special *Golden Goody Award* for Cooper who funded the film
- WHY - The film was made to draw attention to the 80,000 Missing in Action.
- WHERE -*The Director's Guild of America*, Sunset Boulevard, Los Angeles
- WHEN - Memorial Day, 5:00pm

To magnify this story, we worked with our client, *Vanilla Fire Productions* Founder and Director Steven C. Barber. In less than ten days, we wrote a press release, secured event sponsors, and booked media to cover the event. Barber also invited over seventy Marines from Camp Pendleton to attend in uniform, along with actors who actively support veterans such as John Savage ("The Deer Hunter").

National holiday hooks are a very powerful way to attract media attention.

Newsjacking is one of the best ways to secure a media interview. The more you can tie a media hook to current events, the better results you will see in your PR.

Step 4.5 Define HOW You are Helping Others Improve Their Lives

You ALWAYS want to present how you are helping others and/or changing lives in your media hooks. Remember, your job is to gain earned media, and impact stories can provide powerful reasons for a reporter to cover your story.

■ Answer How You Can Help Others in Media Pitches

If you can answer any of these questions in your media pitch, your story will get a lot more attention:

1. Can you solve a problem that saves people time and money?
2. Can you save someone millions of dollars?
3. Can you help someone raise money?
4. Are you raising money or awareness for a cause?
5. Can you help someone rebound after a crisis?
6. Can you reduce family feuds over the holidays?
7. Can you help prevent forest fires?
8. Can you help someone prevent getting the flu?
9. Can you motivate people to make a positive change?
10. Can you help build a financial plan so someone can quit their day job?
11. Are you saving lives, and if so, how?
12. Can you help people find joy, and if so how?

Remember, a story is rarely all about your "cool company". Dig deep here and find ways to help others as an organization in all your media pitches. I could write a whole book on social impact campaigns, and why this problem-solving approach is so important for PR.

Step 4.6 Define Three to Eight Talking Points to Support Your Story Hook

Whenever you pitch the media or schedule an interview, you want to provide talking points that your spokesperson can share. The best approach is to provide three to eight bullets that are simple one-liners. These bullet points can help reporters quickly evaluate potential stories that are competing for their precious air time.

Your job as a PR professional is to make the interview easy for both the media and the spokesperson. Remember, newsrooms tend to be "crazy busy" and the producers are more overwhelmed than most people on the planet. They literally get thousands of email pitches a week and are constantly juggling breaking news stories.

The better your media hook, pitch, and talking points, the more likely the producer or reporter is to cover your story. It's also best to reduce the number of emails back and forth. Try to provide most of the information in your first email. Send limited follow-up emails to reporters to streamline the conversation. Remember, the media is getting bombarded with emails and the last thing they want is ten messages from you.

We have also written the entire script for TV interviews in a question-and-answer format. It's important to note that a script should only be used as a guideline because you want an interview to be a more natural conversation. However, it would be rare not to have a minimum of drafted talking points that your spokesperson can share before doing any interview.

As an example, here are the talking points that we sent to Debbi DiMaggio, her husband, Adam Betta, and the host for the *KGO-AM* radio interview about their new book, *The Art of Real Estate*.

■ *Goody PR* Case Study — Pitch with Talking Points for DiMaggio

Email Subject - Bay Area Authors Launch New Book with DiMaggio Charisma

Potential Talking Points:

- How to win a bid on your dream house (they have won bids with lower offers).
- How to get your house ready to sell with professional imagery, no matter the price point.
- How to choose the right agent who understands marketing (social media and more), is a team player, and has a good reputation in the local market.
- How to stand out as a real estate agent.
- How hyper-local residential real estate is for the Bay Area, and how it differs by region from state-to-state.
- How Debbi DiMaggio is related to baseball legend Joe DiMaggio.

These talking points were focused on how the authors could help educate a broad audience. Anyone interested in buying a home would find these insights helpful. Along with having great tips, the chemistry clicked with the radio host and guests.

Step 4.7 Provide Supporting Media for your Story Pitch

In addition to booking an interview, the producer may ask you for supporting media. This request happens often after an interview is scheduled and is most common for TV. Producers may ask for a book cover image, headshot, logo, and/or press kit documents.

■ Important Note about Email Attachments

It's very important to note that you should NEVER attach anything to an email when sending an initial pitch to a reporter—unless they request it. You may be able to embed an image in a pitch using different email software tools. However, the media does not want to open your attachments unless they know you first. If you send a press release to reporters, always copy the content within the body of the email or send a recognized source link versus attaching anything.

For TV, many times the producer will ask for photos or b-roll video that they can use in the background during the interview. While they do not always use these digital assets, producers often say "send us as many as you can" because they want options. For example, several news outlets used b-roll from *Modern Family* EP Danny Zuker's *TEDx* Talk in the background during TV interviews about his book. Because the *TEDx* Talk was about how Zuker uses *Twitter* to test jokes, it was relevant to his book about a *Twitter* exchange with Donald Trump in 2013.

In all cases, make sure your file names include the people and places in the picture or video. This specific naming of files will make it much easier for the producer to keep your digital files straight.

In a recent *CBS 46 News* Atlanta story about *Warriors Heart Foundation*, the producer asked for photos and b-roll video. We sent ten images and two videos to give them options. As a result, five of these images were in the story, including the company logo, photos of the handmade flags made by veterans at *Warriors Heart*, a headshot of the spokesperson in uniform (*U.S. Air Force* Colonel (Ret.) Chris Stricklin), and a screenshot of his *Facebook* fundraiser page. When this feature interview all came together, the images added great value to an already compelling story.

After you do all your interview preparation steps, it is almost impossible to control what ends up in the final version of the story because, remember, it is earned media. If you had complete control, it would be a paid ad. For earned media, the final decisions are made by the reporter and producer.

What is in your control is giving them options and presenting your story in a clear, concise, and compelling manner. The good news is that 90 percent of producers will ask you for images.

Step 4.8 Test Media Hook A, B, C and Repeat

When you are pitching your story to reporters, it is always best to test different media hooks. You also should not pitch everyone on your media list at once. It is much better to spread out the timing of your pitches. Customizing the media hook based on the outlet, media type and their specific audience is always the best approach.

Test different pitches and see what is working and what is not. The timing of your email or call is also important. For example, you do not want to pitch just before or during the show's airtime for TV or radio.

Similar to sending out press releases, it is better to pitch on a Tuesday, Wednesday, or Thursday because it is the middle of the week. Mondays can be overwhelming with breaking news stories, and by Friday, many reporters are checking out for the weekend.

For your media success, a great email subject line can really mean the difference between getting a story covered or not. Think about what headline you would click to read on social media or your online news apps.

If you are looking for feedback from a free focus group, do not forget that you can go to *Twitter* or *Facebook* and see what people are saying related to a keyword using hashtags. You can also post a story pitch idea or ask a question on social media to see which topic gets the most interest.

For example, if you have a doctor as a PR client, you can go to *Twitter* or any social media site to research headlines. You can find out which hashtags are trending related to your topic, and connect your pitch to relevant and timely topics. For example, when we went to *Twitter* and entered #FluShots, here is the buzz that we found:

■ **Free Focus Group — #FluShots Hashtag on** *Twitter*

Challenge: Let's get our #flushots! I'll go first. I got my shot last week....
and....it did NOT give me the flu. #vaccines #VaccinesWork #hcldr RT
@JoeBabaian

'Tis the season of forced #Vaccinations How did people survive before
#flushots (trick question)? #Nature knows what it is doing, more than
#mankind does. RT @701NDN

#FluShots are government experiments to see if they can predict
viruses as well as a form of population control.

With @TexasHHSC reporting #flu cases on the rise in Texas, now is the
time to get your #flu shot. Here are 5 things @TheDocSmitty wants
you to know about the vaccine RT @CookChildrens

Based on this #hashtag research summary, there are a few possible media hooks. For example, your doctor client can talk about whether you should get a flu shot. If the doctor lives in Texas, he or she can definitely comment on potential causes of flu case numbers being up in that state.

CHAPTER 4 RECAP

Are you now ready to write media hooks that immediately connect with journalists? Do you have new ideas for how to pitch the right topic at the right time? All of these new skills for timely and relevant pitches are an important part of your Media Hook Superpower. Let's look at a recap of what we have covered in this chapter.

Step 4 Action Items — Write Power Media Hooks to Connect with Reporters

1. Write an eight-word email subject with a moving story hook.
2. Define a clear and compelling hook in the first sentence of every pitch.
3. Define the star(s) in each story pitch.
4. Define why the story is relevant and timely.
5. Define HOW you are helping others improve their lives.
6. Define three to eight talking points to support your story hook.
7. Provide supporting media for your story pitch.
8. Test Media Hook A, B, C and repeat.

PR Superpower 4 — Media Hook Superpower

With the media having an attention span of less than eight seconds, your Media Hook Superpower will give you an advantage. If you are lucky enough to get a reporter on the phone, get to the point in one to two sentences. Are you ready?

Chapter 4 — 8-Second PR Challenges

As we close Chapter 4, here are your *8-Second PR* Challenges:

1. What are three compelling media hooks for each of your clients/projects?
2. What will you write in your email subject line to get a reporter to open it?
3. How will the first sentence in your email or phone pitch grab their attention?
4. Who will be your spokesperson—and do they have a moving story?
5. How is your spokesperson/expert or organization positively impacting lives?
6. Does your story pitch include testimonials from your client's customers, and are they willing to speak on camera about it?
7. What type of visuals can you provide to illustrate your media hook?
8. How are you going to use social media to research timely topics and trends?

While you may struggle writing pitches at first, don't give up! Your Media Hook Superpower will take you to new heights. The more you pitch, the easier it will become to develop a story hook that resonates with both the newsroom and your audience. This step is not easy. Resilience and creativity are a must for your Ultimate Media Success.

In the next chapter, we will take a closer look at how to identify and find your target audience and reporters. You can save a ton of time by focusing your PR efforts on people who are more interested in your topic.

STEP 5

Target Your Audience with Media Vision to Laser Focus

"Where focus goes, energy flows."

—*Tony Robbins*

How can you find the perfect media outlet for your story? How do you find the best person who specializes in your topic? Now that you have your brand story and media hooks defined, your challenge is to inspire the right reporter to cover your story. With producers receiving thousands of daily pitches, you need Media Vision that is laser focused to see through walls. PR is a fine art with intense competition so it's important to do a lot of research before contacting a media outlet. You can do this!

> **■ PR Superpower 5 – Media Vision Superpower**
>
> You want to use your **Media Vision Superpower** to connect with the right contact who is genuinely interested in your story. To reach your ideal media, fans, and influencers, laser focus your research to see through obstacles. To enhance this PR superpower, *Google* to find out what your preferred reporters and media outlets are talking about online. Sure, most people would like to be in *USA TODAY* or on *CNN*. However, media placements do not happen magically just because you asked a reporter at a news outlet. You need to pitch the right media hook to the right person at the right time, just to have a chance of your story being published to the public. It is critical to fine-tune this *8-Second PR* Superpower to achieve your PR goals.

In this chapter, we will cover eight action items you can take to enhance your Media Vision Superpower so your story is shared with a maximum number of eyeballs. One media interview can make or break your book, product, or service, so it is important to get this right.

STEP 5 ACTION ITEMS — TARGET YOUR AUDIENCE WITH MEDIA VISION TO LASER FOCUS

1. Clearly identify your ideal target market.
2. Develop your marketing strategy for outreach and promotion.
3. Identify your target audience topics and sub-topics.
4. Research your ideal media outlets and influencers before pitches.
5. Identify ways you can work with brand influencers.
6. Build long-term relationships with media and influencers.
7. Send compelling pitches using best practices.
8. Wait. Revise. Pitch again.

PR SUPERPOWER 5 — MEDIA VISION SUPERPOWER

You can significantly increase your chances of getting a media interview if you are smart about who, how, and when you pitch. Along with reporters, you want to find influencers, family and friends who are excited to share your story 24/7 with their network.

Step 5.1 Clearly Identify Your Ideal Target Market

Before you even start reaching out to any media, research and document your brand's target market. Many make the mistake of skipping this step. Research is one of the most important parts of any marketing and PR planning process. Outlining the demographics for your ideal customer (age, geography, and interests) will help you be much more successful in your media outreach.

You can then match these customer characteristics to reporters who write for them to increase your chances of more publicity. You must know your target market before launching any marketing campaign to avoid wasting your valuable time and money.

Target Market Segment	8-Second PR Tips for Defining Your Audience and Media
Age and Gender	Age ranges and gender can help you identify the right media and social media to use in your marketing strategy. Are you targeting millennials, baby boomers, or everyone 18 to 69? Are you looking for outlets that focus on men or women? For example, a pitch for *Woman's Day* should speak to a different audience compared to a story idea for *Men's Health*.
Geography	We've spoken about the power of getting local media to cover your story first. Think about news outlets close to your office. Ask the spokesperson where they were born, went to school, or work to make connections with local reporters and fans.
Niche Interests	Look for media who write for niche audiences. A niche may include women's interests, health, technology or pets. You will get better results by pitching like-minded reporters or outlets with an engaged fan base interested in your topic. For example, an entertainment reporter for *Variety* is not looking for the same things as a medical reporter for *Everyday Health* or finance columnist for *CNBC*. Pay attention to the niches for your media pitches!
Income	It is also helpful to identify the income range for your ideal clients and customers. For example, if you are promoting a high-end retailer who wants to attract clients making over $250,000 per year, luxury lifestyle magazines such as the *Robb Report* may be perfect.
Profession	Identify media that write for the professions of your ideal customer. For example, if you are looking for successful small business clients with fewer than 500 employees, do your research on this market. Then, pitch media to leading publications such as *Entrepreneur* and *Inc.* magazine who write for this audience.

Target Market Segment	8-Second PR Tips for Defining Your Audience and Media
Influencers	Identify influencers who are recognized experts with big social media followings related to your topic. More people read their news today on *Facebook* than any other social media site. As a result, influencer marketing is an important area for you to add to your overall strategy.

Having the right strategy to connect with your ideal media and demographic will have a major impact on your Ultimate Media Success.

Step 5.2 Develop Your Marketing Strategy for Outreach and Promotion

Before you get started with any media outreach, step back and ask questions. Take a walk, brainstorm, interview your clients, think about the timing of pitches for each type of media outlet, and determine the best strategies for each of your marketing campaigns.

Here are two case study examples of marketing and PR campaigns that *Goody PR* managed with very different target markets.

Target Market Case Study 1 — Tom the Tax Expert – Successful Small Businesses

The first thing we did when working with Tax Expert Tom Wheelwright was to ask about his target market. As the CEO of *WealthAbility*, Wheelwright provides tax and wealth strategy services and education to a specific niche.

AUDIENCE – Wheelwright defines his target market as successful small-business owners, entrepreneurs, and investors. The key word here is "successful" because his tax and wealth strategy services are not cheap. However, the investment is worth it for a sophisticated investor with a complex portfolio of assets.

GEOGRAPHY – For geography, I partnered with his to team to identify seven major cities as key markets for clients, including New York, Chicago, Los Angeles, San Francisco, Washington D.C., Orlando, and Dallas. Wheelwright has clients all over the world in over thirty countries. However, it is helpful for PR and marketing to have his top cities identified.

TOPICS – As a result, we targeted finance, real estate, and wealth reporters who are focused on high-income, small business and investor audiences. For example, Tom can explain how to maximize tax savings by investing in oil and gas, real estate, and business. His target media is reporters who have covered tax and wealth advice tips in *The Washington Post*, *The Wall Street Journal*, *Investor's Business Daily*, *Forbes*, *Realtor.com* and more.

Wheelwright can also educate a broader audience of entrepreneurs on topics such as the most commonly overlooked tax deductions, how to write-off your family vacation, and how to deduct a home office.

Public Relations has been a steady marathon for the past four years working with Tom Wheelwright. While the media hooks, goals and priorities change constantly, the target market for media remains steady. As a result, we are grateful for coverage for this client by *FOX and Friends*, *CNBC*, *FOX 10 News* Phoenix, *CBS 5 News KPHO Phoenix*, *The Washington Post*, *The Wall Street Journal*, *Accounting Today*, *TaxPro Today*, *ABC Radio News*, *NPR*, *710 WOR*, financial podcasts and many other outlets.

Goody PR also pitched a column to the *Entrepreneur magazine* editor for Tom, and he has been writing for their audience for the past two years. Overall, Wheelwright has had over 700 media hits (print, radio, TV, columns and syndicated pickups) and his *Tax-Free Wealth* book has been a steady bestseller ran on *Amazon*.

Target Market Case Study 2 — Sci-Fi Indie Film Director – Film, Sci-Fi and Politics

As another case study example, we worked with an independent film director who released a sci-fi independent film movie. He was the client of a LA-based PR firm, where I was hired as an independent contractor to manage his PR for about one year. On a regular basis, the client partnered with us to brainstorm their top media topics and preferred publications.

Based on the film and client's background, we pitched entertainment reporters who were interested in three key topics. Here is the breakdown for this decision:

AUDIENCE – Even though this movie was a low-budget film that could not compete with blockbuster science fiction films such as *Star Wars* and *Star Trek*, it had a loyal audience already attached. The film was based on the director's popular novel that already had a huge fanbase with a timely political twist.

TOPICS – Sci-fi, politics, and independent film were the main topics for pitching this movie to the media. Our client also wrote an episode for *The Twilight Zone* many years ago, which significantly increased his credibility in the sci-fi world. Based on his experience working on a popular TV series and as a novelist, the media in this niche were much more interested in interviewing him about his sci-fi film.

GEOGRAPHY – This director lived and filmed the movie in Nevada. We used this geography to pitch media in his home market. Because we took advantage of this local media vision, the movie was reviewed in the *Las Vegas Weekly*. The client was also interviewed on the local Las Vegas *NBC News* affiliate *KNSV* about why he chose to film in Nevada.

EVENTS – Event marketing was another part of the overall PR and marketing strategy for this project. This director hosted a red carpet event in Los Angeles, along with movie screenings around the country via *TUGG*. He also spoke regularly at related conferences. A few weeks before each event, we pitched the local media, especially if there was a director Question and Answer session.

CELEBRITY – A well-known actor starred in this indie film, which also contributed to the film's PR success. This star was willing to do media interviews if it did not conflict with his other project obligations. It's important to note that entertainment stories are very competitive, especially if the main actor is not an A-list star. Having a celebrity attached to a project definitely helps with PR, but it does not guarantee anything.

This independent film was harder to promote in Los Angeles because reporters are more focused on mega blockbusters in the theater. When it was later released as a Blu-Ray DVD, I helped with that PR too, which extended the campaign.

As a result of the team approach with the client and PR agency, we were fortunate to have this low-budget film covered in an average of five stories per month steadily for one year. National media included *FOX News Red Eye, Ron Paul Channel, David Webb Show, Hot Air Radio Show, The Washington Examiner, Larry Elder Radio Show*, and more.

Step 5.3 Identify Your Target Audience Topics and Sub-Topics.

When you develop your media outreach strategy, you also want to clearly identify your topics and sub-topics. While most experts want to be interviewed on *CNN*, thousands of reporters and producers work for *Turner Broadcasting*. Your job is to clearly identify a client's expertise, find the right producer, build a relationship with them as someone who can provide credible sources, and then present timely pitches.

Clients can have multiple topics and sub-topics, depending on their current campaign, product, or service. Each time you reach out to the media or influencers, you want to keep their core audience in mind. The more relevant the pitch is to the reporter, the better your chances are of getting an earned media story.

For example, we pitched four story ideas to *USA Today* magazine (which is different from *USA TODAY*) for our *Goody PR* clients. In response, the editor requested three story submissions. Their guidelines ask for a 2,000 word story that addresses a problem and provides solutions. The magazine topics include "politics, ecology, education, business, media, literature, science and religion." Because our clients are mostly small business CEOs, we pitched topics related to investing, taxes and entrepreneurship. With 256,000 paid subscriptions for this magazine, I recommended writing these stories.

Here is a comparison of two campaigns for the same client, using very different approaches for media and influencer outreach:

Client: Debbi DiMaggio, Top One Percent Realtor, author, and philanthropist	Campaign 1: Real Estate Book Launch	Campaign 2: Philanthropist Make-A-Wish Type Campaign
Campaign	Book launch: *The Art of Real Estate*	Summer Birthday Make-A-Wish Type Campaign sponsored by local Philanthropist
Topics	Real estate, realtors, buyers, sellers, book reviews, publishing industry	Charity, social impact, real estate
Sub-topics	Consumer tips, Realtor tips	Fashion, San Francisco, Bay Area, Lady Diana (Debbi's role model; both had summer birthdays)

Client: Debbi DiMaggio, Top One Percent Realtor, author, and philanthropist	Campaign 1: Real Estate Book Launch	Campaign 2: Philanthropist Make-A-Wish Type Campaign
Events	Book signings, real estate speaking events and real estate conferences	Event 1: Fashion Day for 25-yr-old with chronic illness who loved fashion, and Debbi loved fashion too. Event 2: Make-A-Wish Birthday Party at a local charity who helps children with terminal illnesses.
Geography	National and local	National outreach on social media. Focused PR pitches more on local media with two Bay Area events.
Influencers	Realtors, real estate industry organizations	Social good influencers sent happy birthday video wishes. Local fashion retailers in San Francisco donated store space and new clothes for Fashion Day. My digital marketing class made a video with "Happy Birthday" messages in 10+ different languages.
Key Results	*Unique Homes* profile, speaker at *Inman News* National Conference for Realtors, column in *Inman News*, *Real Estate Radio Live* (twice), local TV news profile story, consumer advocate talk radio station interview and more.	*ABC 7 News* Bay Area story about Make-A-Wish type birthday party, *My Social Good News*, local paper coverage, birthday videos posted by key influencers, and local recognition by clients for giving back.

Step 5.4 Research Your Ideal Media Outlets and Influencers before Pitches

When you research your media outlets and influencers before pitching, you have endless ways to check their backgrounds with the internet. While there are many sophisticated tools to find media quickly that you can purchase for large fees, basic research is a must for your key media. Here are eight suggestions for researching reporters and fans:

■ *8-Second PR* **Media Research Tips**

1. *Google* the topic and desired media outlet to find the right reporter covering your topic.

2. Search the topic and click "News" on *Google* to see who has recently written about your area of expertise, and then pitch them.

3. Search keywords using #hashtags on social media. For example, try entering #SanFrancisco, #SocialGood, and #RealEstate on *Twitter* or *Instagram* to find people interested in these topics.

4. Create a list of key influencers and reporters, and then start following them on *Twitter*. Pay attention to the topics they are posting in tweets and in their coverage. You may find a summary of their stories on websites such as *Mud Rack* for journalists.

5. Share key media and influencer posts with compliments on social media. If you consistently like, retweet, and reply/comment on a reporter's stories (especially on Twitter where it is easier to reach a stranger), your support can go a long way when building media relationships.

6. Search on *LinkedIn* for a reporter's profile and industry groups that you can join in niche areas.

7. Attend conferences related to your key topics to meet reporters and influencers in that space.

8. Ask people for suggestions for what outlets and reporters to contact. This request may sound obvious, but many skip it! Many PR professionals will guard their contact list, and that is understandable. However, many will give you media outlet suggestions. You can also join a PR professionals group on *Facebook* where industry leaders regularly share advice tips.

Reporters spend a lot of time on their stories, and they want to be heard just like you do. It is important to read what others are saying, and then show that you are listening by giving their posts some love (Re-tweet, Share, Like). Obviously, you don't want to go overboard and be perceived as a stalker, but you can make contact with reporters on social media.

When you go to conferences, do not forget to engage with your target media and influencers. You can tweet and post using @username and hashtags related to your media topics and sub-topics.

To connect with reporters and influencers during conferences, post photos on social media with multiple hashtags before, during, and after conferences. Click on these hashtags and Comment on other posts by people who share similar interests. For example, I went to the *National Publicity Summit* in New York City to pitch media, and have been able to connect afterwards with several reporters and authors who attended simply by looking up other posts with #NationalPublicitySummit on *Instagram*.

Step 5.5 Identify Ways You can work with Brand Influencers

How many times have you logged onto social media and asked your friends "What do you recommend for a great new [fill-in-the-blank]?" This Word-of-Mouth marketing now plays a major role in any promotional plan. You must target the right influencers in your marketing, PR and social media campaigns.

> **■ The Power of Word-of-Mouth Marketing**
>
> According to a *Nielsen Report* (2015), people are 90 percent more likely to trust a brand recommended by a friend. People are four times more likely to buy if the product is recommended by a friend (*Nielsen*).

There are many ways that you can partner with brand influencers to magnify your story on social media, at a conference, at a party, book signings, and at family dinners. The Word-of-Mouth marketing opportunities are endless. Let's look at some examples and suggestions for reaching influencers.

INFLUENCER MARKETING — PRODUCT GIVEAWAYS

One of the best marketing approaches can be product giveaways with the hope that the influencers will share your brand on social media and/or write an earned media story about it. In this case, no one is paid to talk about the product, making the results more genuine and authentic.

INFLUENCER MARKETING CASE STUDY — *SUNDANCE FILM FESTIVAL*

Some of the best examples of product-giveaway marketing can be seen at the *Sundance Film Festival* in Utah. This annual event is hosted by the *Sundance Institute* and is known for defining "cool." Brands such as *Southwest* and *Chase Sapphire* have spent huge budgets to rent space on Park City's Main Street during the festival that gets flooded with over 40,000 film fans for ten days every January.

Companies spend a fortune to rent space and participate in festival events to get celebrity and influencer photos with their products and/or recommendations. For example, *Eddie Bauer* gifted their *MicroTherm® StormDown Jacket* at their "Adventure House" on Main Street for three years in a row.

This *Eddie Bauer* Adventure House lounge and gifting suite attracted major stars and influencers such as *Academy Award* Winner Allison Janney (*I, Tonya*), Jeffrey Tambor (*Transparent*), John Legend (music legend), Molly Shannon (*SNL*), Gina Rodriguez (*Jane The Virgin*), *Golden Globe* Winner Alexander Skarsgard (*Big Little Lies, TrueBlood*), James Marsden (*X-Men*), Ethan Hawke (*Training Day*), Jason Segel (*How I Met Your Mother*), Nikki Reed (*Sleepy Hollow*), Chris Pratt (*Guardians of the Galaxy*), Ron Livingtson (*Office Space*), Kristin Wiig (*Bridesmaids*), Jack Black (*School of Rock*), and Kevin Smith (*Clerks*).

Full disclosure, as an entertainment journalist, I received this *Eddie Bauer* jacket as a free gift. Because I truly loved this jacket, I posted it everywhere on social media and included it in my Top 10 Gifts at *Sundance* recap.

Starting in 2017, the *Sundance Film Festival* cut way back on many of these gifting suites to focus the festival more on film. However, you will still find major brands sponsoring festival events. For example, *DOVE® Chocolate* and *Refinery29* cosponsored a "Women at *Sundance*" brunch hosted by the *Sundance Institute* in 2017.

Many products continue to be gifted to influencers at other major entertainment conferences (*Comic-Con, Vidcon, NAPTE*) and awards season events.

INFLUENCER MARKETING AT INDUSTRY EVENTS — *CES* CONFERENCE

Many brands incorporate influencer marketing into major industry conferences like *CES (Consumer Electronics Show)* in Las Vegas, Nevada. For example, Calvin Lee @MayhemStudios has almost 100,000 Twitter followers and is recognized as a key influencer in the digital space. Calvin often posts gifts on social media that he receives (*Sony* cameras, new technology and more). Along with gifts, many influencers like Calvin may have their travel expenses paid by a sponsor.

What makes Calvin Lee so authentic is that he is a graphic artist by day and influencer 24/7 who openly shares his personal life online. Calvin posts regularly about everyday things that make him very relatable. For example, his Twitter feed has tweets about birthdays, dinners, family, photographs, and industry events. Calvin also posts portrait photos that he takes regularly on social media. He has built a powerful influencer brand, and his photography has been seen on *ABC7 KABC News* in Los Angeles.

Along with gifts, brands like to offer invitations to "exclusive parties" and/ or a sneak peek of "exclusive content." For example, the television and movie studios will often invite key influencers to preview parties of their work to build buzz around projects.

There are social media management tools to help brands identify key influencers in their space based on geography, number of followers and key interests for this purpose. Brands will then reach out to influencers on *Twitter* with special invitations and offers.

PAID INFLUENCER MARKETING —
THROUGH INFLUENCER MARKETING AGENCIES

There are also paid influencers for marketing campaigns now. Yes, there is currently a business where you can hire a *YouTube* star or social media influencer to create a video or piece of content about your brand for a fee.

There are different levels of influencers and compensation. Some social media stars are invited to events and given gifts as a thank you. Others are paid to tweet and post during a live broadcast. For example, TV show casts are often now asked to tweet live during the airing of an episode. Other celebrities such as Kim Kardashian are reported to get paid up to $10,000 for one tweet for a brand like *Shoedazzle* (*HuffPost*).

Several of my fellow *Social Media Club Los Angeles* board members run influencer marketing agencies. They connect major brands such as *Nordstrom* and *Abercrombie and Fitch* with influencers online for this purpose. For more information, search online for influencer marketing agencies such as *Reelio, Viral Nation, RG Pacific,* and *Tiny Sponsor.*

In addition to influencers marketing, reporters now get paid to write sponsored content stories. You may receive a request for an expert quote for a brand sponsored story. In this case, pay careful attention to whether your brand or PR client's values are aligned with the company paying for the story.

Step 5.6 Build Long-Term Relationships with Media and Influencers

Once you are fortunate enough to connect with a reporter or key influencer, you want to keep building upon that relationship. As in any long-term partnership, you have to find the right balance and right timing to keep in touch with each person.

> ### ■ Case Study - Long-Term Media Relationship – *ESPN Cover Your Assets*
>
> We have been fortunate to build a long-term relationship with Todd Rooker, who is the producer and host of *ESPN Cover Your Assets show* in Minneapolis, Minnesota. It's a one-hour 50,000-watt radio program on Saturday mornings that covers a wide range of financial advice topics.
>
> As a result of building a long-term relationship with Todd, I have been fortunate to book the eight *Rich Dad Advisors* on his show, plus Robert Kiyosaki (Author of "Rich Dad Poor Dad", the number one financial book of all time). And in several cases, I was able to book these guests multiple times.
>
> Along with being a Radio Show Host, Todd's *Rooker Financial Consulting* business advises clients who are in a "financially challenged situation" to ensure it never happens again. I have enjoyed calls with Todd learning about how he has positively helped clients change their lives by investing in real estate.
>
> In addition to these interviews, Rooker has graciously offered to record PSAs for *Goody PR* clients and play them during his show. I cannot emphasize enough our gratitude to Todd for this extra support.
>
> If you meet a reporter who is this passionate about your topic and helping others, go to great lengths to build a long-term relationship with them.

Switching gears to entertainment reporters, our PR colleague Doris Bergman has hosted awards' season events in celebration of the *Emmy Awards* and *Academy Awards* for years in West Hollywood. What she does most brilliantly is build long-term relationships with entertainment reporters and celebrities who consistently attend these events.

Influencers keep coming back because Bergman provides a relaxing experience with genuine people who don't have an "attitude", a gourmet lunch at the trendy *Fig and Olive* restaurant on Melrose Place in West Hollywood, and popular gifts for everyone approved to attend. The media, celebrities, and brands all play an important role in making these events a huge success.

If you are trying to get media coverage for your product, you always want to think about the reporter's point of view when pitching. Most reporters who attend Bergman's events do it because they really care, not because of pay. What most people do not realize is the greatest cost to a blogger or columnist is time. A great event recap can take five-ten hours to write, edit photographs and video, and share on social media.

For influencer marketing, step back and ask what public figures, celebrities, and trendsetters care about the same topics?

■ Case Study — Influencer Marketing for *Jukin Media* Launch

When we partnered with *Jukin Media* to develop their first PR campaign, we identified a list of key digital influencers in Los Angeles to invite to their holiday launch party. Because *Jukin Media*'s business was focused on acquiring viral video clips to sell to major TV shows (*Comedy Central, TODAY Show, MTV Ridiculousness*, and more), digital industry influencers were a perfect match.

We sent out personalized VIP invitations to key influencers whom I knew from networking events in Los Angeles. We also enlisted sponsors to provide products for gift bags for these influencers. The majority showed up, tweeted about the new company, and posted the event on *Facebook*. This influencer marketing approach contributed to putting *Jukin Media* on the map in the entertainment capital of the world!

For this event, *Jukin Media* also partnered with Rob Dyrdek, star of *MTV Ridiculousness*, to support his charity at this launch party. Dyrdek was busy shooting a *Super Bowl* commercial so he could not make the event. However, we obtained permission to promote his name, brand, and charity (*Rob Dyrdek Foundation*) in association with this successful launch.

At the time, *Jukin Media* had about ten employees in Hollywood in a small office. Today, they are in a much bigger space with 150+ employees in West Los Angeles. The company is now recognized as an industry leader in the Silicon Beach tech community. (P.S. They just partnered with *Snapchat*.)

Step 5.7 Send Compelling Pitches using Best Practices

Once you have your Media Vision developed, start sending custom email pitches to the media and influencers using our *8-Second PR* best practices. As a quick review, here is a summary of key points covered so far:

■ *8-Second PR* Best Practices for Pitches

- Keep It Simple.
- Write a compelling email or press release headline using eight words or fewer.
- Include an active verb in your headline (*launches, announces, changes*, etc.)
- Get right to the point in your first sentence because you have only eight seconds to grab their attention (revise the first sentence several times to get this right).
- Provide the Who, What, and Why, plus How you are helping others in your pitch.
- Add When (date and time) and Where (the address) for events or contests.
- Provide three to seven bullets as potential talking points.
- Include a short bio for each spokesperson and organization.
- Include media experience for a spokesperson to add credibility by showing they have been quoted in print as an expert, and/or interviewed on radio or TV.
- Ask a question at the end.

In addition to these best practices for pitches, pay attention to the title of the person receiving your email. You want to send pitches to a Writer, Columnist, Freelancer, Special Assignment Reporter, Features Producer, Guest Booker, Talent Booker, News Producer or newsroom. Pitches that are emailed directly to a Host are often overlooked, especially if it is a major media outlet. Chances are good that Shepard Smith (*FOX News*) and Brian Williams (*MSNBC*) are never going to open a pitch email.

CASE STUDY EXAMPLE — PITCHES FOR BUZZ PONCE CHARITY BIKE RIDE

We were fortunate to work on a PR campaign for Baby Boomer Buzz Ponce, who rode his bicycle cross-country to raise awareness and money for *Warriors Heart Foundation*. Buzz rode from California to Florida, and we got the best media response at his start in San Diego. Three local TV news stations requested interviews with Buzz within three days. To get this trifecta result, we made the media hook timely, local, and inspiring.

While pitching this story idea sounds easy, it was not. Remember, the newsrooms are overloaded with thousands of daily pitches competing for limited airtime. We definitely had to pitch several times in different markets, along with testing subject lines, pitch timing, and follow-up. As an example, here is the pitch subject line and first paragraph that resulted in multiple interview requests:

■ Winning Pitch - 3 TV Interview Requests in 3 Days

Email Subject: Pitch – Leaving May 1 – Why San Diego Author is Riding 3,100 Miles For *Warriors Heart Foundation*

Hi X,

As a potential timely story for **X**, 70-yr-old San Diego native and author Buzz Ponce (*A Long Ride*) is leaving in two days (May 1) from the Oceanside Pier and can discuss **Why he is Bike Riding 3,100 Miles Coast-to-Coast to Support Military, Veteran & First Responder Healing and *Warriors Heart Foundation***. With Camp Pendleton nearby, the recent strain on San Diego Firefighters, and Buzz being born in San Diego, there are several great local connections here.

What was most surprising about this pitch response is that the email was sent on a Sunday. While our best practice guideline is to send pitches on Tuesday, Wednesday or Thursday, Buzz was leaving in two days so we could not wait. We had been pitching the San Diego media for a few weeks with no reply. However, Buzz arrived in San Diego from Phoenix, Arizona, on Saturday night to prepare for the trip. Being physically there on Sunday and the urgent email subject line all contributed to getting this mega response.

Step 5.8 Wait. Revise. Pitch Again.

Once you have identified your topics, relevant media, key influencers, and sent out your pitch, you are now waiting for feedback. Breathe in, breathe out, and let the reporter or influencer digest what you are saying.

You can always follow-up with phone calls and ask for feedback. While most reporters will not answer the phone, it is worth trying and leaving a short voicemail. If you make enough calls to your target market reporters, eventually, someone will answer the phone and give you feedback.

If you get really lucky, a reporter will get back to you soon after they receive the pitch. If they are serious about interviewing you or your client, trust me, they will call.

Fortunately, many times over the past ten years, reporters replied within one hour of a pitch for *Goody PR* clients. It is always a good feeling to get a quick reply.

However, this rapid response to media pitches is rare. It is more likely that you have to send seven different pitches with a variety of media hooks to a reporter before he or she actually covers the story or says "No". Honestly, most media and/or influencers will never even open the email. Some major publications will not even accept "unsolicited" pitches.

There are days where you get no replies at all. You need a lot of patience and stamina in PR so you never give up. There were many pitches for Buzz's charity bike ride sent to media in Phoenix, Arizona (where he lives now) and no one ever replied.

As a best practice, PR professionals should wait a few days or even a few weeks before pitching via email or the phone again. The time of day depends on what and whom you are pitching. For example, if you are pitching something about an event related to the American Flag, and it is the week of July 4, you probably want to pitch every day. If your topic is not tied to a specific event or headline news, then it is much better to spread out the timing of your media pitches and influencer campaigns.

CHAPTER 5 RECAP

Are you ready now to pitch to your key media and influencers with their topics, geography, and timing in mind? Here is a quick summary of your key take-aways for this chapter:

Step 5 Action Items — Target Your Audience with Media Vision to Laser Focus

1. Clearly identify your ideal target market.
2. Develop your marketing strategy for outreach and promotion.
3. Identify your target audience topics and sub-topics.
4. Research your ideal media outlets and influencers before pitches.
5. Identify ways you can work with brand influencers.
6. Build long-term relationships with media and influencers.
7. Send compelling pitches using best practices.
8. Wait. Revise. Pitch again.

PR Superpower 5 — Media Vision Superpower

With your new Media Vision Superpower, you will now be able to find the right audience for your story and build long-term relationships to increase your earned media and Word-of-Mouth marketing.

Chapter 5 — 8-Second PR Challenges

As we close Chapter 5, here are your *8-Second PR* Challenges:

1. Who is your ideal target market for customers and media? Consider interests, income, geography, and more.
2. What three publications are on the top of your media outlet wish list?
3. If you do PR, who are the top three preferred reporters for each client?
4. How can you build long-term relationships with your preferred media?
5. Who are key influencers for your client's product or service?

---

6. How can you build long-term relationships with key influencers in your areas of expertise?
7. What are five different ways to pitch the same thing?
8. What days and times are you going to try pitching each outlet?

Your Media Vision Superpower will help you see through obstacles and find creative ways to stand out. A big part of your job is brainstorming ways to reach the media in different ways. Don't get discouraged if you get no response. It's just like being in sales. You have to keep going back, and never give up pitching until you get a "No".

In the next chapter, we will take a closer look at how you actually take a media request and turn it into a home run by getting a story published.

STEP 6

Make Your Interview Take Flight to Score Mega Media

"Be so good, they can't ignore you."

—STEVE MARTIN

A re you ready to learn how to get your media interviews over the finish line? What are the PR secrets for booking an interview and getting it published? Most people have no idea what it takes to secure a TV, radio, or print interview, and honestly, that is why many hire a PR professional or agency instead of doing it themselves.

Earned media coverage rarely happens by pure coincidence. In this chapter, we will provide inside scoops for how to turn an idea into an earned media story. It's a lot like playing baseball, and your Interview Flight Superpower will help you score mega media in national news outlets such as *CNN*, *FOX News* and the *TODAY Show*.

■ PR Superpower 6 – Interview Flight Superpower

Many authors and experts do not realize that just because you get an interview request, it does not mean a story will be published. Your **Interview Flight Superpower** can help you follow-up consistently to score mega media hits! When you receive an interview request from a reporter, you're up at bat. However, even if they do the interview, it might not be shared. Like scoring a run in baseball, getting in the headlines is a process that takes skill, endurance, and patience! Every time you get a media opportunity, you want to be prepared to advance

> the story around the bases until it crosses home plate as a published story! If you stumble, get back up again until you score earned media using this *8-Second PR* Superpower!

In this chapter, we will cover eight action items to get your brand in the headlines.

STEP 6 ACTION ITEMS — MAKE YOUR INTERVIEW TAKE FLIGHT TO SCORE MEGA MEDIA

1. Get back to media within one hour of an interview request.
2. Make it really easy for the media.
3. Coach your PR client on what to expect and next steps.
4. Turn your talking points into a Q-and-A script for the producer.
5. Send the interviewer great visuals in support of your story.
6. Be available 24/7 if the media needs anything.
7. Follow-up to move your story around the bases and score.
8. Genuinely thank the reporter and their team.

PR SUPERPOWER 6 — INTERVIEW FLIGHT SUPERPOWER

When a reporter calls or emails you to schedule an interview, it's your job to actually get a story published. You can make a media request take flight as long as you have a Wow Story, are responsive, and follow up. It all starts with the brand story that you defined in Chapter 1 and have been fine-tuning throughout this book. Once you get a request from a reporter, it is a baseball game of advancement until your story gets to home plate!

Because America has been recognized as the free press leader of the world, using baseball is the perfect analogy for a PR tips book written in America. And this freedom of the press is something we should all value like these three former U.S. Presidents.

> ■ **3 U.S. Presidents - Freedom of The Press Quotes**
>
> *Our liberty depends on the freedom of the press, and that cannot be limited without being lost.*
>
> —Thomas Jefferson

Absolute freedom of the press to discuss public questions is a foundation stone of American liberty.

—Herbert Hoover

We are not afraid to entrust the American people with unpleasant facts, foreign ideas, alien philosophies, and competitive values.

—John F. Kennedy

Scoring media is truly a sport that requires skill and strategy. Let's take you around the bases with our winning *8-Second PR* strategy that we have used over and over again.

Step 6.1 Get Back to Media Within One Hour of an Interview Request

If you are fortunate enough to get an interview request from a reporter, you should be jumping up and down celebrating. Out of the hundreds, if not thousands, of emails and calls they receive every day, you just won a Golden Ticket for a potential story.

To make sure that you own that opportunity, it is best to respond immediately to the media. My goal is always to respond within one hour, especially for TV interviews. Because many reporters send email requests rather than call, PR professionals need to be constantly checking email.

We are fortunate to have smartphones now that go with us everywhere. It makes it so much easier to stay in touch and monitor media requests remotely. However, you can still miss an opportunity if you are not paying attention.

For example, when I was still promoting my dating book in 2006, I remember missing a national TV interview opportunity because I sent a blocked phone number to voicemail during a coffee meeting. Because I did not immediately check the voicemail or email, the *FOX News Channel* producer simply picked up the phone and called the next "dating expert" in their database of potential guests.

You can bet that I now check voicemail from anonymous phone numbers at warp speed, along with scanning my email inbox regularly.

Fortunately, this interview request was for my dating book and not a *Goody PR* client. By the time I started my boutique marketing agency in 2008, I had much better technology and systems in place in order to be very responsive to the media.

Based on your time zone, you may also need to adjust your media monitoring patterns because most major outlets are based in New York City. Living in California, we often get requests from East Coast reporters early in the morning.

If it is for a radio or print interview, it is usually not as urgent and can actually wait a few hours. However, the bigger the media outlet, the more important it is to get back to the reporter ASAP! Sometimes they do need an immediate confirmation, so pay attention to the details in all requests.

■ *Goody PR* Case Study Examples – 3 Last Minute Interview Requests

Marketplace - We received a last-minute radio interview request from *Marketplace* for Tom the Tax Expert. The reporter wanted a soundbite for a nationally syndicated show that was being published later that day. Fortunately, we were able to reach the client in the airport before he flew overseas. While the producer only included a few sentences from Tom, this interview aired across the country on 800 radio stations with over 14.8 million unique listeners over a week (Source: *Marketplace*).

CBS Atlanta - For another client, we received a call at 6:30 a.m. PST from a *CBS Atlanta* TV producer, who wanted to interview our client that day by 1:30 p.m. EST (10:30 a.m. PST). We immediately called the client to work out the logistics (time, place, talking points). This client was in a very important annual budget meeting, and fortunately, his senior management team agreed to break for this TV interview because it was that important. In the end, it was a home run for everyone involved! The segment ran that evening and the following morning for a total of four times with three promotional plugs. It featured my client's name, his charity's name, and the name of his company. The Calculated Publicity Value, according to a *Nielsen* Media Report, was over $28,000. (Note: This publicity value is very high for local news, which is usually worth $3,000 to $10,000 for a two-to-three-minute segment.)

CNN - In a third scenario, I received a "maybe" interview request from *CNN Newsroom with Brooke Baldwin* for *Modern Family* EP Danny Zuker. The pitch was that Zuker could talk about how politics and pop culture were overlapping, and the timing was perfect because it was very close to the 2018 Midterm Election. With so much breaking news, the producer explained they would not be able to confirm until the

---

morning of the show, which airs 11:00a.m. - 1:00p.m. PST. When we woke up at 7:00 a.m. PST, we got the "green light" for the interview. Our client was asked to go to the *CNN Los Angeles* office, and had a split screen interview with the host who was in New York. Everyone scrambled to make this interview happen, and it was over six minutes on national TV!

To make it even easier to track interview requests, we set up a separate email for media only. This approach lets us quickly monitor requests, and they do not get lost. If you are doing PR for your product or a client, I highly recommend setting up an email for media requests only.

Step 6.2 Make It Really Easy for the Media

As shown in the *CNN Newsroom with Brooke Baldwin* interview example, you always want to make it really easy for the media to interview you or your client. While everyone has schedules and lives, you need to keep in mind that the media are overwhelmed with juggling requests and breaking news. If you are fortunate to get a call from them, you always want to move quickly and be as flexible as possible. Do not hesitate and try to make it happen based on the media's schedule. And please leave your attitude at the door because they are saying, "We want to tell your story to the world."

The exception rule for "drop everything for the media" would be for a request from a reporter with an outlet, blog, or podcast that is not well-known and/or they have no social media following. You can also pass if the outlet is not be a good match for your target audience. It's okay to politely say "No" if the stars do not line up.

Whenever we get interview requests from unknowns, we do extensive research for clients before saying "No". If it is a small outlet, there still may be a good reason to do the interview. For example, if the reporter also writes for a major publication (*Forbes, The Hollywood Reporter, CNBC*), it may be worth doing the interview to build a relationship with the reporter.

While making TV interview requests a top priority sounds reasonable to most people, we cringed when a client declined a great opportunity by saying; "I am going to pass because it is not convenient". In another case where a TV crew was ready to go, the client replied; "I need to take a nap."

In the first scenario, this TV interview "pass" was probably a loss of about $20,000 in Calculated Publicity Value because it was in a major market. And yes, I wanted to scream because this decision not only hurt the client's relationship with the media outlet, it made our company look bad. Because TV reaches the most people and is the hardest to book, it is always best to find a way to "Yes" to a TV producer.

In a recent *Thrive Global* story, I was grateful that my advice tips were quoted in a story about ways to make the interview process easy for the media.

■ Make It Easy for the Media — Published in *Thrive Global*

You always want to make to make it easy for the media by providing a short bio in every pitch for your client with their name, title, URL, previous media experience and your contact information. If a reporter gives you a time for an interview, respond quickly and try to make that time work. Making an interview process easy for the media will build relationships and result in more repeat interviews. They have enough to worry about with so much breaking news, so make everything easy for them!

—Liz H Kelly

In addition to being responsive, you always want to have an electronic press kit ready in a folder that supports your latest pitch in case a reporter asks for more. If you get a last-minute interview request, a fast response can be critical, so have this information ready.

■ Top 10 Electronic Press Kits Items

1. Personalized cover letter/email
2. Customized talking points
3. Question-and-Answer script (one page only, five to seven questions)
4. Spokesperson title and bio for the interview
5. Most recent press release and/or recent media
6. Website to be used during interviews
7. Images (headshot, logos, book cover)
8. Video (b-roll of client, product, or service, if available)
9. Book copy (if applicable)
10. Your contact information

A hard-copy press kit may also be requested by mail if you have enough time to get it to them before the interview. For a book launch, a snail-mail press kit and book copy are more likely requests. To ensure that this process is seamless, use *FedEx* or a service where you can track who signed for a package. I recommend using bright-color folders that include your business card.

For a recent evening interview with *CNN International*, the producer initially said they did not need advance book copies. They changed their mind the morning of the interview. Of course, we wanted to jump to make it easy for them, especially since this was a global TV interview. As a result, we scrambled to print press kits and drive them to Hollywood mid-day to avoid traffic. It really helped that we had an electronic press kit for the book already prepared in a folder on our computer that could be easily customized.

After scrambling for this *CNN International* producer, *Goody PR* printed ten press kits so they were ready to go the next time. The only part that needed to be customized was a cover letter.

Step 6.3 Coach Your PR Client on What to Expect and Next Steps

To be able to get back to the media quickly, you also need to coach your clients on this rapid-response approach, especially for TV requests. Whenever you get a call or email for national media or TV interviews, your job is to find out ASAP when the client is available, where the client is located (time zone and place), and then coordinate with the producer to make it happen.

To make sure your interview takes flight, work with the reporter, your client and/or their assistant to confirm the details. Recently, we had a last minute radio interview request from *Dr. Drew Midday Live with Lauren Sivan* for a client. Because the interview time was three hours later on the same day, we called, texted, and emailed the spokesperson. When there was no response, we texted other people at the client's company until we got everything set up. Fortunately, the interview was confirmed within about an hour and the producer held the interview timeslot open.

Here is your interview checklist with steps:

■ Interview Flight Confirmation Checklist

- Confirm the interview date, time, and location.
- Confirm the approximate length of the interview.
- Get instructions and/or directions for each party regarding the format (phone call, *Skype, Zoom Video Conferencing*, or in person.)
- Confirm the topic and talking points with the reporter and the client.
- Coach new clients or media spokespeople on best practices for TV, radio, and print interviews.
- If TV, provide general media coaching tips for a first-time TV appearance.
- Once the interview is scheduled, confirm everything is set up with both parties (interviewer and interviewee).
- If the interview is live, listen live online and/or tape the interview.
- If you are not with your client for a media interview, always ask them for feedback so you can manage the follow-up. Remember other than live TV, whether a story gets published may depend on the follow-up. Ask "How did it go?" and "Did they say when the story will be published?" These specifics can save everyone time and build stronger relations because the reporter does not have to repeat things.

It is also good to create a system for interview requests. Our preference is to have one main contact for each *Goody PR* client, even though most people have team members that play vital roles. If your client has an executive assistant, it's very important to work closely with him or her. Make sure you have their cell phone number for last minute requests. You always want to build a strong relationship with the team, and explain your process for the best results.

For PR professionals, ask clients how they prefer to schedule calendar requests for interviews too. Some *Goody PR* clients want *Google Calendar* appointments set up with reminders. Others have their own internal calendar management system. And some have an assistant who manages their schedule using *Outlook*. The only thing that matters is that everyone is on the same page and follows the process.

In the past ten years of doing marketing and PR full-time, I've been fortunate to have only seen this confirmation process get messed up twice. I wish it never happened, but I did drop the ball on one interview change request when a family member was in the hospital. In the second case, the radio host completely forgot an interview scheduled a month earlier. Our mistake was not double-checking with the interviewer a few days in advance. So, while these planning steps may sound obvious, they are all really important for interviews.

Step 6.4 Turn Your Talking Points into a Q-and-A Script for the Producer

Another really important part of the interview flight process is to write talking points that can be easily turned into a script. We've talked about this action item previously, and it is so important that we want to emphasize it here with examples.

When you write the talking points, they are meant to be teasers versus the whole answer. It is also helpful to include numbers (reporters love lists with numbers). For TV and major radio interviews, it may be better to use a Q&A format. You have to use your best judgement based on everyone involved (the producer, reporter and your client).

■ *Goody PR* Talking Point Examples

- How to tell your story in 8 seconds.
- 3 Ways to Thank a Firefighter.
- Top 3 impacts of new *Tax Cuts and Jobs Act of 2017* on Small Business.
- Why taking a flu shot is not a must.
- Why long-term recovery programs for 90 days are much better than 30 days.
- Top 3 best practices for TV interviews.
- Which superheroes can fly.

In several cases, we have also written out the entire script for the client and the reporter. This extra preparation can make you a PR hero because reporters are so overwhelmed all the time that many appreciate the draft.

During a recent *KTLA Channel 5* News Los Angeles interview, we sent eight Questions and Answers to the producer for a timely book interview. Four anchors interviewed the author at their main desk, and the team used almost our exact list of questions. The more people involved in an interview, the more important a script can be.

Of course, any media interview never goes exactly as planned, but talking points and a script draft can provide focus and save a lot of planning time on all sides (your client's and the reporter's).

■ *Goody PR* Case Study – Why Q&A Scripts Matter

One of our biggest PR wins was a national TV story on *FOX and Friends* for five co-authors for the book *More Important than Money – An Entrepreneur's Team*. The book was written by Robert Kiyosaki (*Rich Dad Poor Dad*), his wife Kim Kiyosaki (*Rich Woman*), and his eight *Rich Dad Advisors*. Four of these co-authors were in New York City to promote this book at the national *Book Expo America*, and this TV appearance all came together as a huge PR win—with a few hurdles.

We pitched the story with different angles for about three weeks, but the producers were very hesitant to have so many guests together. Even though I knew the producers from a previous client interview, there was no guarantee of a TV interview happening.

When I finally wrote out the entire script, including an introduction by Robert Kiyosaki of his *Rich Dad Advisors*, and then one to two entrepreneurial tips from each expert on the team, the producers agreed to proceed. They could finally visualize the interview with a script in front of them.

Coordinating with the *FOX and Friends* producers, Robert Kiyosaki, *Rich Dad Advisors*, the *Rich Dad* team and their guests resulted in many home runs for all!

Fortunately, this *More Important than Money* panel interview ended up being six minutes on national TV (when most TV interviews are two to three minutes). And the Calculated Publicity Value, according to a *Nielsen* Media Report, was approximately $136,000.

You cannot buy that kind of publicity. What got this *FOX and Friends* interview over the finish line was the script! Bottom line, you have to make it easy for the media. Ask questions about what they need, and write a script draft if you think it will help.

Step 6.5 Send the Interviewer Great Visuals in Support of Your Story

On top of writing meaningful talking points and a great script, you always want to send the reporter some great visuals that can add to the print, radio, or TV coverage. We've covered this topic already, but it really is so important that it is added here again.

Remember, all interviews should educate and entertain because people want to feel like they are gaining valuable information. Visual learners like graphics, pictures, posters, and other visual aids (*Source: Reaching the Visual Learner,* William C Bradford, 2004.)

For Baby Boomer Buzz Ponce's 3,100-mile bike ride for charity from Oceanside, California to the St. Augustine Beach Pier near Jacksonville, Florida, the TV producers wanted photos and video.

The reporters LOVED Buzz's story because it was both inspiring and heartwarming to see a man who was about to turn 70 years old ride cross-country to help heal veterans and first responders struggling with addiction and PTSD.

■ *Goody PR* Case Study — Buzz Ponce Finish Line Interview Visuals

To document, Buzz Ponce's 3,100-mile coast-to-coast bike-ride finish in Florida, we were fortunate to book two TV local news interviews (one the day before, and one at the finish line). To illustrate his long journey benefiting *Warriors Heart Foundation*, we provided the TV producers with these visuals:

1. Image with map of Buzz's bike ride route from his website.
2. Photo of Buzz with a smile along the California coastline bike route.
3. *Warriors Heart* logo with black-and-white image of veterans and active military.
4. *Warriors Heart Foundation* logo.
5. Photo of Buzz at the *Warriors Heart* ranch in Texas with his bike and the team.
6. Photos of Buzz at the St. Augustine Beach Pier with the *Rotary Club of St. Augustine,* who were there to greet him.
7. Video of Buzz leaving the Oceanside Pier in Oceanside, California.
8. Videos of Buzz finishing his bike ride and dipping his tire in the Atlantic Ocean at the St. Augustine Beach Pier.

While these TV segments were nowhere near the PR value of the *FOX and Friends* story, the sentimental value was much higher. Buzz and *Warriors Heart* founder/president Josh Lannon (who is also Buzz's stepson) will value this local news coverage for a lifetime.

■ Image Quality Requirements for TV and Print Interviews

Photographs and graphics should always be high-quality images for TV and print stories. What this means is the image should be at least 500KB or higher, and preferably one to three MB. If you do not know what this file size means, *Google* it or hire a marketing professional to help you.

In all cases, images are a must for media interviews! You can also hire a graphic artist or professional photographer to develop your digital assets. It is really that important!

Step 6.6 Be Available 24x7 if the Media Needs Anything

Because the media never sleeps, you need to make yourself available 24/7 for last-minute changes or requests. While I try to avoid having my team work on weekends to maintain a life balance, you are never completely off when doing PR.

To make sure the *FOX and Friends* story about the new book *More Important than Money* actually aired, I set my alarm for one Saturday at 4:00 a.m. PST for a 5:20 a.m. PST scheduled interview. I wanted to be available to troubleshoot any last minute rescheduling requests. Fortunately, this segment aired on time. However, with so much breaking news, you can never be 100 percent sure your story will actually be aired.

When I was promoting my dating book, I had a national TV interview cancelled two minutes before it was scheduled because of breaking news. It was like a scene out of the movie *Broadcast News*. I had asked a couple whom I helped to find love to be part of the interview. This couple took off work and were in the studio in Washington D.C. I was 3,000 miles away with a microphone and earpiece set up in the Los Angeles satellite studio for *FOX News Channel*. Then I heard someone in my earpiece say, "Please pick up the phone." It was the NYC producer saying, "Your segment just got cut due to breaking news out of Iraq."

Fortunately, I was able to recover the story within twelve hours, and the interview ran the next day. However, the happy couple in Washington D.C. were not willing to take another day off from work and risk the chance of the interview being cancelled again. I was relieved to find another couple in Los

Angeles and made the interview happen. This recovery process was not easy and required focus, patience, and a lot of follow-up.

Many radio interviews are also live and may require some flexibility for crazy hours. For example, many of our clients get booked at 5:00 a.m. PST for East Coast morning shows. For these requests, you always want to research the host and show thoroughly to see if it is worth the extra effort.

The media never takes holidays either! For example, we booked two local TV news interviews on the Fourth of July for the same client because of a related breaking news story. I was on a sailboat in Marina del Rey, had my smartphone, and was able to reach the client. Everything just lined up in this case, despite most of the country not working that day. Thanks to smartphones, anyone can manage media interviews from anywhere and reach clients for last-minute requests.

Step 6.7 Follow-up to Move Your Story Around the Bases and Score

With all of these Interview Flight Superpower tips, here is the most important thing to remember. Getting a media interview aired is like playing baseball. Your job as a marketing and PR professional is to get the earned media interview over home plate so the world can see your client's story.

You may run into obstacles in this *8-Second PR* Baseball Game. You could miss your turn at bat, strike out, or get stuck on one of the bases. It is important to navigate this process with confidence and patience. Yes, there is strategy and skill in this game of getting an earned media story published.

■ *8-Second PR* **Baseball Game — Scoring an Earned Media Story**

GET UP TO BAT – You are nowhere in the earned media game until you get an interview request. If you are lucky enough to get a request from a reporter who wants to share your story, congratulations, you are up at bat. If you do not get an interview request, keep reinventing your media hook until you get out of the dugout.

ADVANCE TO FIRST BASE – To get to first base, you want to secure the interview by getting it scheduled. To advance, coordinate with both parties to confirm the date, time, and place for the interview. At any moment, your interview might get cancelled, so it is important to act quickly and get the timeslot booked on everyone's calendars.

ADVANCE TO SECOND BASE – When you actually have the interview, you have now advanced to second base. If your interview is LIVE, you will immediately score and advance to home plate! If the interview was pre-taped or was a phone interview, your primary job changes to follow-up.

ADVANCE TO THIRD BASE – If the interview was not live, follow-up will advance your story to third base. It is all about follow-up at this stage, and you want to avoid being stuck on third base forever. (Yes, this can happen, so master your follow-up!)

SCORE AN EARNED MEDIA STORY– If you are lucky, the interview was live, and you immediately scored an earned media story. If it was not live, avoid getting stuck on third base or, even worse, never get the story published. Your PR mission is to score earned media interviews with the right media by getting stories published. To get there, it's a balancing act. In all cases, don't burn bridges and know when to let go. Always listen to your gut instincts and their feedback closely.

We have sadly seen clients get around the bases, get stuck on third base, and never score. Some interviews or columns have taken six to nine months before being published while others never got selected for publication. When an interview gets stuck during this follow-up process, it can be a big bummer for you and the client.

For example, we scheduled an in-person interview for a client at a major financial publication in New York City. It's been six months since their face-to-face meeting, and no story has been published. The reporter changed the approach by saying it may be an expert mention in a story instead of a feature article. I have not given up, but I do admit this part of the process is very frustrating.

However, sometimes things are just out of your control. A reporter may get a new job, the editor may not like the story, and/or the client's story is not compelling enough.

Getting up to bat and doing an interview that is never published is rare, but it does happen. For example, we had a crew from a local TV news station cover a *Rich Dad Hawaii* event in Honolulu, but the story never aired. Fortunately, we had other local TV stations cover the same event, and those stories got published.

In another case, we had a PR client who was interviewed about their "life story" in December 2017 for a print article, but the story did not run until the following June 2018. After six months of follow-up, multiple reviews of a 3,000-word story, and overcoming hurdles because the original publication (*Huffington Post*) cut off contributors, this profile story was FINALLY published in *Thrive Global*.

Your worst-case scenario is a client who is rude or has "an attitude that they are better than others" with a reporter. In this situation, not only is the story never going to be published, you may not get another interview opportunity with that reporter. Big egos can kill a story fast. Remember, everyone is important, including the expert, reporter, the executive assistants and the entire team at a radio or TV station. You want to emphasize to your clients that being grateful goes a long way with reporters.

This *8-Second PR* Baseball Game process is just like dating. If you act too aggressive or desperate, your story might get cancelled. If you get a reporter on the phone, show empathy for a busy schedule and ask questions to learn more about the best next steps. In all cases, gratitude and patience will help you score far more wins than losses in this *8-Second PR* Baseball Game!

Step 6.8 Genuinely Thank the Reporter and Their Team

No matter how big the media outlet, you always want to thank reporters before, during, and after an interview. We've also talked about this point earlier in this book, but want to say it again because it is SO important! After you score an earned media story, it is easy to just move on and forget to say thank you.

We cannot emphasize enough how important it is to thank the reporter and mention their entire team afterwards. A short and sincere email can go a long way and increase your chances of being invited back. I worked with a PR mentor who used to write hand-written thank-you notes to journalists after every major interview. These thank-you notes repeatedly landed his clients on major national TV shows such as the *TODAY Show*, *Good Morning America*, *CNN*, and more.

After the *FOX and Friends* story for five coauthors, we handwrote six thank you notes to the producers. While this took extra time, the snail mail approach helped us stand out in their avalanche of digital correspondence.

Adding positive comments on *Facebook* posts for the story is another great way to acknowledge the reporter's work. Your response shows you care, have read their article, and are sharing online.

Remember, many reporters are getting paid zero to almost nothing, and receive very little appreciation for their work. Journalists are human beings just like you—so ALWAYS be courteous and say thank you! It's free and easy, so just do it!

CHAPTER 6 RECAP

Overall, this chapter is about scoring interviews and building long-term relationships with reporters. Your goal should always be to get as many earned media stories published as possible, along with getting second interviews.

Step 6 Action Items — Make Your Interview Take Flight To Score Mega Media

1. Get back to media within one hour of an interview request.
2. Make it really easy for the media.
3. Coach your PR client on what to expect and next steps.
4. Turn your talking points into a Q-and-A script for the producer.
5. Send the interviewer great visuals in support of your story.
6. Be available 24/7 if the media needs anything.
7. Follow-up to move your story around the bases and score.
8. Genuinely thank the reporter and their team.

PR Superpower 6 — Interview Flight Superpower

With your new Interview Flight Superpower, you will now be able to get your interview scheduled and published for the world to see.

Chapter 6 — 8-Second PR Challenges

As we close Chapter 6, here are your *8-Second PR* Challenges:

1. What tools can you set up to help you reply to a reporter within one hour of an interview request?
2. What are you going to include in an electronic press kit?
3. How are you going to set expectations with your clients so they can help you reply to media requests with warp speed?

---

4. What Q-and-A scripts do you have ready for your clients to send TV producers?
5. How often are you going to contact the media if your story gets stuck on third base with continual follow-up?
6. When do you know it's time to give up on the story follow-up?
7. How can you show your appreciation and support for a story on social media?
8. How are you going to thank reporters after a story is published?

Your Interview Flight Superpower skills can help you score more earned media interviews for clients and/or yourself. Now, you know how to follow-up, which is a huge part of your job and Ultimate Media Success!

In the next chapter, we will talk about what you can say to make your interview messages hammer home. Ready?

Hammer Home Your Interviews to Magnify Media Results

"People have an infinite attention span if you're entertaining them."

—JERRY SEINFELD

Do you know how to get to the point immediately? Do you know how to use emphasis statements when sharing your story? Do you know how to use the power of threes to highlight key points? When you are given the opportunity to have a media interview, you want to make every word count. Reporters want to talk to people who can deliver great content, so add a little magic to your message!

It takes a lot of steps to get to an interview, so make the most out of every opportunity! Most reporters want their guests to keep it simple, deliver a compelling story with confidence, and look good if it is an on-camera interview. It all matters, so you or your client need to be prepared when you get to share your message with the world.

If the person being interviewed thinks all they have to do is show up and deliver knowledge to their audience, think again. While there is some value to improv, hammering home messages in media interviews is much more complicated than it looks.

> ### ■ PR Superpower 7 – Interview Thunder Superpower
>
> Messaging is a PR art that you can master with the **Interview Thunder Superpower**. When you get the opportunity to do an interview with a reporter, make sure to be GRATEFUL first and then be prepared to hammer home your messages. For TV, print, radio and podcasts, you want to move your audience with powerful soundbites. Use emphasis statements and examples of how you have helped others to quickly draw attention to your story. Just as thunder can make you stop what you are doing and look up, you want people to stop multi-tasking and focus on what you are saying. Your thunder will be impacted by your ability to deliver great content with a memorable delivery. For TV, your tone of voice, non-verbal expressions, props, and what you wear all matter in a very visual world. If you speak with confidence and conviction from the heart, you will make lasting impressions using this *8-Second PR* Superpower!

In this chapter, we will cover eight action items to enhance your Interview Thunder Superpower. By delivering your message with confidence, it can go viral to the right audience and receive a great response:

STEP 7 ACTION ITEMS — HAMMER HOME YOUR INTERVIEWS TO MAGNIFY MEDIA RESULTS

1. Practice your talking points with 8-second messaging in mind.
2. Be grateful, flexible, and early with the media.
3. Dress for success for TV interviews.
4. Speak from the heart with a genuine interest in others.
5. Speak with clarity and conviction, even if you get thrown off.
6. Be entertaining and interesting (tell me something I do not know).
7. Give real-life examples of how you helped others.
8. Smile. Breathe in. Breathe out.

PR SUPERPOWER 7 — INTERVIEW THUNDER SUPERPOWER

An interview is showtime for your brand story! Your audience will decide in the first eight to fifteen seconds if they will continue watching, listening, or reading your story. Get excited! Make some noise! And most importantly, make your audience fall in love with your story!

Ready? You can do this!

Step 7.1 Practice Your Talking Points with 8-Second Messaging in Mind

To secure this media interview, you have defined the brand story, sent out a press release, written a powerful media hook, and now you have a reporter who wants to interview you or your PR client. You made it to first base just by getting the interview scheduled. You want to be ready to score big now when the reporter starts asking questions.

To prepare, one of the best things you can do is practice saying your key talking points out loud with emphasis. Use the talking-points draft as a guide. A written script does not always sound natural (which is why someone reading a speech can sound really awkward). You always want to deliver your message with conviction on the phone or on camera. By saying the words out loud, you can make changes so it sounds more authentic based on your personal style.

If this is a TV interview, there is a lot more preparation. The interview will happen so fast that if you are not ready, you will be saying "could of, would of, should of" with regrets for a long time afterward.

You can also practice saying your key talking points with a friend, your PR representative, and/or hire a professional media coach. The bigger the media, the shorter time you will probably be allotted to tell your story. Being clear and concise are not easy so do not take shortcuts on your preparation, especially for a TV interview.

Bottom line, you always want to get the reporter's and/or the audience's attention right away. Remember, attention spans are shrinking so first impressions mean everything. Just like thunder and lightning happen in a split second, you must immediately gain their interest.

For all types of media interviews, we encourage our clients to start sentences with emphasis statements. If you watch cable TV news, look for the media pros who use these types of phrases:

■ *8-Second PR* Emphasis Statements

The most important thing is . . .

The number one thing is . . .

Liz H. Kelly

The top three things are . . .

Remember the top two things about X are Number one . . . and Number two . . .

If you only remember one thing, don't forget to. . .

To illustrate the importance of these emphasis statements, here are two TV interview soundbite examples from way back when I was promoting my dating book, *Smart Man Hunting*:

■ TV Interview Examples — Emphasis Statement Soundbites

TV Interview 1 – During a national talk show interview on *NBC* about first dates on *The Other Half* (guys version of *The View with Dick Clark, Mario Lopez and Danny Bonaduce)*, I was asked by actor Dorian Gregory (*Charmed*); "Why do first date disasters happen?" Our opening reply was; "Well I think the biggest cause of dating disasters is fear. People are anxious. Their fear of the unknown, fear of disappointment, and number one fear of rejection."

TV Interview 2 – In another local TV news interview on *ABC* 7 Los Angeles about internet dating profile tips, we shared, "The number one mistake is they write too much about themselves. They write something too general, and so I try to help them put some personality in the profile."

Step 7.2 Be Grateful, Flexible, and Early with the Media

To ensure media success, you always want to be early, grateful, and flexible for print, radio, and TV interviews. While we may sound like a broken record, you cannot afford to go through all the steps to get here and then blow the interview! Set appointment reminders for interviews and review your notes before every media opportunity.

GRATEFUL – As soon as you meet a reporter, the first thing you always want to say is THANK YOU for interviewing me! If the reporter took the time to select you from thousands of emails, it is like winning the media lottery. I cannot emphasize enough the importance of being grateful versus being a prima donna. Check your ego at the door for all media interviews. The producer and reporter are in charge. Get excited, and work with him or her to make it their best interview ever!

FLEXIBLE – Always be flexible with the media because they are juggling a lot of stories at once. While you want to avoid rescheduling an interview at all costs, the media may ask you to move the date and time. The producer often cannot control breaking news, and things do come up for everyone. In all cases, be positive and flexible. The minute you start being high maintenance, they can easily go find someone else to interview about your topic. For example, we were asked to reschedule a TV interview twice over a two-month period for a *Goody PR* client in Los Angeles. In this case, we stayed flexible by working with the producer and client to make this story happen!

EARLY – You also want to be early and prompt for interviews. It is not as critical to be early with a print interview because it is usually a phone call and can be rescheduled more easily if needed. However, if it is LIVE radio or television, you always want to be EARLY. Most producers will request that you dial-in five minutes early for live radio and be in the studio 30 to 45 minutes early for TV.

Another reason to be early for an in-studio interview is because there is usually high security at media stations. If it's your first time visiting, you don't know exactly where you will park and how long it will take you to check-in. In one case, our name was not on the guest list as the PR contact for a client so the front gate sent our car to a "holding area" until they could reach the producer. Fortunately, we were fifteen minutes early, got confirmed within ten minutes and made it by the "designated arrival time" (45 minutes before the segment). It all worked out despite the minor delay.

LIVE RADIO INTERVIEW TIPS

The good news about radio is that you can usually do the interview from anywhere, as long as you are prepared. For radio, it is very important to pay attention to the instructions about whether the interview is via phone, *Skype, Zoom,* or another technology that the host prefers. When we confirm a radio interview, the detailed instructions are always included in the email confirmation and/or appointment request.

If you are a radio show guest, always review your notes again about fifteen minutes in advance for remote interviews to avoid any delays and dial-in early. You do not want to be fumbling at the last minute trying to figure out the logistics and talking points because it may impact your tone and delivery.

During a recent *Money Radio 1510 AM Business for Breakfast* talk radio interview, the interview was scheduled for five minutes with Tax Expert Tom Wheelwright. (Keep in mind, the bigger the station, the shorter the interview.) In this case, Tom was ready to go with his notes, and it showed in the delivery. The topic was "6 Misunderstood Tax Deductions". When the host turned the microphone over to Tom, and said, "I'll let you go through them," Tom described each deduction with clarity, conviction and easy-to-understand examples.

The other important thing to know about remote radio interviews is that you need a high-quality phone or internet connection in a QUIET place. We cannot emphasize this enough! While it might sound so obvious, we have booked so many clients who did not take the sound quality seriously.

Several clients were booked for one-hour radio interviews, which is really long. This show costs the host about $20,000 to produce one episode, and they spend a lot of time finding sponsors. When one of our clients got disconnected a few times during the live interview, it was embarrassing. Honestly, it is just inconsiderate not to plan ahead and test the connection. These sound quality challenges are bad news for the radio show host, your audience, your delivery, your brand and the PR professional who booked it. Avoid this scenario!

For another national radio interview with *NPR*, a client asked the host, "Can you call me back because I am busy now?" I was not on this call, but the client said they had a brief discussion, and he then agreed to do the interview. While they recorded the interview, you can guess what happened next. This interview NEVER aired on this national radio program. The host would not reply to our multiple follow-up emails, phone calls, and apologies. This casual and inconsiderate approach to a national reporter is really bad form on multiple fronts. It not only makes the guest look self-absorbed and ungrateful, it also reflects poorly on the PR company who scheduled the interview. This scenario was not good.

If a PR agency wants to book other clients on this national radio show, this spokesperson just damaged the long-term relationship with that reporter for everyone. OMG! UGH! SO FRUSTRATING! (Reminder: Leave your ego at the door and be grateful when reporters call for interviews!)

In a more positive scenario, our client was interviewed in-studio live on *Dr. Drew Midday Live with Lauren Sivan*. It's a 3-hour daily talk radio show on *790/KABC* Los Angeles, along with the ability for anyone to listen live online. Because the client arrived early to the studio and breaking news was slow that day, the hosts kept him on the air for almost forty minutes. The sound quality was excellent because it was managed by the radio show's production team. This interview was a home run for the client and *Goody PR*. As a result, we booked another client twice on the same show for different topics.

LIVE TV INTERVIEW TIPS

Through the process of doing PR for my first book, I learned that the top two rules for live TV interviews are 1) wake up at least two hours in advance so you have high energy and no puffy eyes and 2) arrive at the station at least 30 to 45 minutes early. Most TV stations or shows will have a waiting room for guests to relax in until it's time for their segment. It might be the front lobby or a green room for bigger shows.

Waking up two hours in advance can be a real challenge if it is an early morning interview. For example, my first TV interview about my dating book was at 5:50 a.m. on *WMAR-ABC* in my hometown of Baltimore, Maryland. This interview time meant a 4:00 a.m. wake-up call (which can be a major challenge for a non-morning person). Fortunately, it was Thanksgiving weekend, and I was staying with my parents. They turned on all the lights and TVs and got me moving. In other cases, such as San Diego's *NBC 7 KNSD*, I would book a hotel room right across the street and get up at 3:30 a.m. for a 5:30 a.m. interview (double ouch!).

For national TV interviews, many shows have hair and make-up artists on-site, so they might want you to arrive an hour before the interview.

■ Don't Try to Move a TV Interview Due to Traffic!

In a rare case, a *Goody PR* client got stuck in traffic before a local TV news interview, and it was a real challenge to move the time around with the producer. While traffic snarls happen, you always want to plan way ahead so that you are on time for TV. It IS a HUGE, BIG DEAL to move a TV interview because every second is scheduled! In this case, the interview almost got cancelled completely.

TV producers book their shows by the minute, so give them the courtesy of always being early. They are juggling their team, talent, advertisers, and ratings, so make it easy for them by being an awesome guest on and off camera.

You want your interview to be beyond great and result in "thunder." Remember, this is the showtime you have been waiting for to share your story with the world. If you are late, you will be stressed, which will show in your delivery. If you mess up the producer's schedule, you may never be invited back. Yes, things happen in life that cannot be avoided. However, leave really early and make it a priority to always be on time for live TV interviews. Enough said.

Step 7.3 Dress for Success for TV Interviews

If you are fortunate enough to have a TV interview, you always want to dress for success. Visuals are SO important for television. While you can do a print or radio interview in bed in your pajamas, you are on center stage for TV.

If you are a PR professional, it's important to coach your clients on what to wear and share tips on non-verbal communication. Media coaching tips, drafted scripts, role plays, talking points, and props are all your friends for TV and video interviews.

If you are the author or spokesperson, you cannot afford to show up for a TV interview without wearing your best look and smile. It is really that simple. There is no shortcut here. Get your hair done, get a manicure, wear your favorite color, choose business casual clothes, get sleep and smile!

If you are getting ready to do interviews for a new book, business, or event, consider getting a style consultant. For my first book launch, a consultant reviewed the best colors and styles to wear for my skin tone and hair. This honest advice was a huge help and is highly recommended to anyone with on-camera interviews.

If it is the last minute and you have a low budget, go to *Nordstrom* to have a makeup artist test what looks best on you. For my first TV interview, I went there, and the makeup artist shared extra tips for TV. For women, they recommended going heavy on the makeup and wear eyeliner. The *Nordstrom* professionals can also help you with styles, but I recommend taking a friend for honest feedback on what makes you look great.

Here are some of our Dress for Media Success Tips that we email our *Goody PR* clients in preparation for TV interviews:

> ### ■ *Goody PR* Dress for Media Success Coaching Tips
>
> - The most important thing to remember is to smile and be passionate about the topic because you are the main visual.
> - Wear "business casual" in most cases.
> - Wear solid-color clothes versus patterns.
> - Wear your favorite color or clothes that make you feel good inside. Your confidence will be naturally beaming as a result.
> - Avoid wearing black, white, or red on TV. These colors are not good on camera, and you must avoid them. When I see these colors on TV, I cringe.
> - If you are a woman, wear bright colors. Long sleeves are also better on camera versus a sleeveless dress or blouse. Remember, you are going business casual (unless it is a red-carpet event and everyone is wearing gowns).
> - If you are a man, a navy jacket and light blue or neutral color shirt are best. Avoid wearing a black or white shirt, so there is some contrast.
> - Relax, look at the interviewer, and consider it a conversation with the reporter instead of memorizing a script.

For example, bright fuchsia is a great color for women on TV. When my friend asked me "When did pink become your favorite color," I explained that it was after my first national TV appearance. When I wore pink on *NBC*'s talk show *The Other Half*, the producers praised me for wearing the pink, and I was hooked.

Watch what others wear on TV to see what styles you like best. It is also helpful to watch a program in advance of an interview to learn about the reporter and show. What you wear is important so pay attention to this detail!

Step 7.4 Speak from the Heart with a Genuine Interest in Others

One of my first media coaches explained that it is very important to show empathy for others during interviews. For my dating book, I hired three different media coaches over my five-year promotional campaign. Each one gave me different advice. Showing empathy was one of the most important tips.

If you come across as if you know everything, you will lose some of your audience right away. Your best bet is to acknowledge the challenges and problems that you want to help people overcome.

For example, it was important to be relatable for my dating book, *Smart Man Hunting*. To connect with the audience, I would start off interviews by saying things like "dating is hard" or "it's not easy to find the right guy." Simply by saying these statements in the beginning of an interview, you can win the attention and respect of your audience.

■ **TV Interview Examples — Empathy Statements**

During my national *FOX News Channel* interview about *Smart Man Hunting*, we were asked "What is a man code"? Our reply was; "Well I started making up these codes at parties in Los Angeles because we needed comic relief. Dating was so painful that I had to make up a new shorthand for women."

These empathy statements were very genuine because I was actively dating in Los Angeles, and there were many challenges. All I wanted was to find was a "Bachelor Available" (one of my *Smart Man Hunting* Man Codes) who was emotionally available, attractive, and would not run when I said the word "relationship." People laughed because this statement was sadly so relatable.

Anyone who acts as if they understand dating completely will instantly lose credibility because relationships are so complex. I also shared a lot of Do's and Don'ts for dating with reporters based on interviews with thousands of singles looking for love. Any interview will lose its magic if you only talk about you. Always think about how others feel about your topic, how your insights can help them, and avoid rambling.

In another scenario, we did PR for a General Practitioner Doctor in Palm Beach, Florida. To help others, we booked the doctor on many interviews about the Ebola epidemic in 2014. During these interviews, he discussed the likelihood of this deadly disease reaching the U.S. and admitted that many people were scared. The headlines were definitely making people very uneasy, and they were looking for answers. The doctor's genuine interest in helping people came across on camera. As a result, he kept getting invited back for more TV, radio, and print interviews about this breaking news topic.

Building trust with reporters and your audience can help anyone drive home a message in a media interview. Show empathy, compassion and a genuine interest in others for the best response.

Step 7.5 Speak with Clarity and Conviction, Even if You Get Thrown Off

Along with looking and feeling great, you want to hammer home your messages during media interviews, even if you lose your train of thought. I usually advise clients to practice the top three things that they want to say over and over again, and then the other talking points will come out naturally.

■ TV Story Case Study - Amma "The Hugging Saint" Honored

We were humbly honored to recognize Humanitarian and Spiritual Leader Mata Amritanandamayi, better known as Amma "The Hugging Saint" with our *Golden Goody Award*, at the *LAX Hilton*, during her annual Los Angeles tour. When *KCBS-TV* showed up to cover the story, we lost the reporter with over 3,000 people there. We had to focus on the award presentation with our team instead.

The ballroom was filled with an international audience waiting to see Amma, and we worked with her team to follow the proper guidelines for greeting a living saint.

To keep our speech simple and heartfelt, we decided to thank Amma for her *Embracing the World* charities and mention three of her widely recognized qualities.

When someone mentioned that they saw us on TV, we were pleasantly surprised to learn *KCBS-TV* had done a feature segment. The anchor told the story based on the press release with the exception of our soundbite:

"This is for Amma for her worldwide humanitarian charities, selfless love, compassion and life of service."
                          —Liz H Kelly, Goody Awards Founder

We share this example to highlight Amma's great work, and emphasize the power of threes on TV. Producers are often looking for a short soundbite only, and this sentence worked for them.

If you are not familiar with Amma, Google her name to learn more. Her charities have contributed over $60 million in free medical care for the poor since 1998 (Source: amma.org).

Liz H. Kelly

If you can deliver your top three points with emphasis statements, clarity, and conviction, you will master your *Interview Thunder Superpower*!

A TV producer is not going to risk putting someone on camera unless they really know their stuff because, a lot of times, you will go into auto-pilot during a live interview.

■ Media Rock Star: Steve Schmidt in Soundbites

One of the best media rock stars that we've seen on TV is Communications and Public Affairs Strategist Steve Schmidt. As a Republican, turned Democrat, he brings many great insights to the table from both sides of the isle. He worked on political campaigns for President George W. Bush, as well as the 2008 presidential campaign for then Arizona Senator John McCain.

When asked about *The White House* communications team member mocking a then dying Senator John McCain, Schmidt commented on national TV, "John McCain's valor, his heroism, his love of country,...He's a giant for the ages. He's a living legend, a soldier, a peacemaker...The greatness of John McCain is not dispensed by this *White House*. What her comments show is the viciousness, the cruelty, the meanness, and this culture of bullying."

Watch for Steve Schmidt on the news or search *Google* for his videos. He is a media soundbite pro!

Most of the time you will walk away from a TV interview saying, "What did I just say?" You literally go into a zone, which is why practice and preparation are so important.

Even if you cannot remember your script draft, you can remember to use emphasis and empathy statements upfront—and then focus on your top three points.

If you really lose your train of thought or are thrown off, simply say, "That is a really good question" to buy yourself a little time. Always keep smiling. Never let it show if you are caught off guard. Media interviews are somewhat like a piano recital. Piano teachers will tell students that if you make a mistake, just keep playing because no one will really notice. It's the same thing in TV and radio interviews, just keep going with confidence, even if you say something that was not perfect.

As a quick reference recap, here are some Media Coaching Messaging Tips as reminders for print, radio, or TV interviews.

■ 8 *Goody PR* Media Coaching Messaging Tips

1. Draft 3-7 talking points or bullets with key things to say. Use the list as a guideline rather than memorizing so you sound natural.
2. Focus on your top three points when practicing and say them out loud in front of a mirror before the interview to see if they sound natural.
3. Keep answers short (one to two sentences) so you get to the point immediately for TV and radio rather than using a detailed script.
4. If possible, give a 1-2-3 in one of your answers. For example, the top three things that you want to do are X, Y, and Z. These statements are much easier to follow, and you want your audience to pay attention.
5. Use sixth-grade vocabulary on TV because you are talking to the masses and want to use the same level of vocabulary that works best in most major newspapers.
6. Try to use the name of your company, book, or product one to two times naturally in your answers. For example, mention a product as an example of how it helped someone so that it does not sound like a commercial.
7. Be prepared for the unexpected. No media person is going to follow a script exactly, so remember to listen to the host and think of the interview as a "conversation" rather than a speech.
8. Focus on looking at the interviewer rather than the camera. Leave it to the camera person to get the right shots, unless you are told to look a certain direction.

For example, for the *FOX and Friends* national interview, we worked with the *Rich Dad Advisors* to draft a script because there were five people being interviewed on a panel. Each guest was asked to share one advice tip for entrepreneurs. For real estate advisor Ken McElroy, here is what we drafted versus what he said.

■ TV Script versus Interview – *FOX and Friends*

For Ken McElroy – *More Important Than Money* Book Interview

SCRIPT

Scripted Question:
What is the number one mistake you see with businesses when it comes to real estate?

Scripted Answer:
The number one mistake real estate investors make is that they **do not use debt to get ahead.**

There is good debt and bad debt, and you want good debt. If you borrow money and spend it on something that goes up in value, that is good debt.

You can build massive wealth in real estate if you learn how to use good debt.

TV INTERVIEW – WHAT WAS ACTUALLY SAID

Anchor: What is the number one mistake that you see with businesses when it comes to real estate, real estate investing?

Ken McElroy: So, what I see is that they do not use debt properly. There is good debt and bad debt, and bad debt is like credit card debt. And that is what a lot of people do. It is very expensive. Good debt is actually using debt to buy assets (like real estate).

While what Ken actually said on TV is not an exact match to the script draft, it did not matter. It came across as an authentic answer with conviction. A confident tone and delivery are what really matter most on camera. If Ken had to come up with the answer on the fly, he would have been fine because he knows his stuff. However, the preparation made this interview flow much better with the panel-style format. The script ensured that everyone got to make a key point and was clear, concise, and compelling.

Step 7.6 Be Entertaining and Interesting
(Tell Me Something I Do Not Know)

Another must for media interviews is to be both entertaining and interesting. You want to tell the world something they do not know. Otherwise, why bother reading or listening to your interview? Being both entertaining and interesting takes preparation, unless you are a natural born comedian.

When I work with our *Goody PR* clients, we are always brainstorming for things that make them different. Reporters want to know how their message stands out from others doing similar things.

■ The Magic in *Smart Man Hunting* — The Man Codes

What made my dating book, *Smart Man Hunting*, such a media magnet was the 26 A to Z Man Codes for the different personality types. There are TONS of dating books out there, but no other book had these funny man codes as a compatibility guide in an easy-to-read A-to-Z guide.

From the *All Sports Fanatic* to the *Zodiac Zealot*, each code has a movie and true story example that producers, hosts and reporters loved to cover during interviews. For example, our *Nourishing Nester* man code description compared this personality type to Brandon Roth's character in the movie "Superman Returns" because of this superhero's random acts of kindness.

When I appeared on *The Other Half* the first time, I was the "dating expert" on a panel talking about what a woman should do because her boyfriend of three years had not proposed. While Dick Clark thought there was no problem with dating for a long time, I jumped in to say, "He's a *Relentless Renter*. He will rent forever and never buy! So, she should dump him!" And then Danny Bonaduce agreed with me. (*Relentless Renter* was another one of my man codes, and they were great for TV soundbites!)

Honestly, the man codes were the thunder, lightning and magic that made *Smart Man Hunting* stand out with over 500 media hits for one book.

In a national TV interview on *FOX News Channel*, the whole interview focused on these man codes. Entertainment Host Bill McCuddy asked me about several codes with fun movie examples. As a great visual, they played the movie clips as b-roll video (and yes, this was scripted so they were ready). For example, the "Hello Good-bye Guy" is Owen Wilson's character in *Wedding Crashers*. And even though this interview aired on the July 4th holiday, the book hit the *Amazon* bestseller list for a week.

To create these man codes, it took months of brainstorming, interviews with couples in great relationships, and research to find the right movie examples. Think about what type of examples you can use to educate and entertain your audience.

Using interesting and short soundbites is not easy when the cameras are rolling. With practice, you will get better each time you have a TV interview. Think about what makes your story different and then highlight this thunder.

Step 7.7 Give Real-Life Examples of How You Helped Others

Along with being entertaining, it is also critical that you can show how you have helped others. Remember, one of the best ways to get media coverage is by showing how you are making a positive social impact.

One of the main reasons we love working with *Warriors Heart* is the great work they are doing to help warriors overcome their "War At Home." It is a very special team making a difference, and many have very inspiring stories. For example, one of the best spokespeople is Former Special Forces veteran and *Warriors Heart* co-founder Tom Spooner. He served 21 years in the *U.S. Army*, including 12 combat rotations and 40 months in combat. After almost taking his own life and struggling with chemical dependencies, he understands first-hand the challenges that many of the warrior population face. To give back, Spooner chose to dedicate his life to helping fellow warriors get back to work and their loved ones with a solid long-term recovery plan.

In another case, Kevin Costner and his band *Modern West* headlined a Thomas Fire Benefit to raise money for those impacted by the devastating 2017 fire in Ventura, California. In addition to Kevin, *GRAMMY* Winners, singers and songwriters Colbie Caillat and Olivia Newton-John also performed at this benefit concert. This Thomas Fire Benefit was supported by 180 sponsors (*Bank of Sierra, ACM Academy of Country Music Awards*) and 120 volunteers (including *Goody PR* who volunteered based on a request from PR pro AnnFlowerPR.com). This fundraiser concert was sold out, and raised more than $730,000 (*Ventura County Star*) for the community to rebuild. This event also attracted major media coverage, including *Entertainment Tonight, EXTRA, KCBS, KEYT, US Weekly*, and more.

What many people do not understand is that a really great media story is never about you. It is about how you helped, impacted, or changed the lives of others.

Step 7.8 Smile. Breathe In. Breathe Out.

In all media interview cases, it is really important to smile, breathe in, and breathe out. Does this mean that you will never get stage fright? Absolutely not! What it means is that there are things you can do to help you relax and reduce your nerves.

SMILE INSIDE OUT

For all media interviews, your emotions tend to show up on camera. It is best to be constantly working on loving your life. If you feel good inside, this feeling will come across during both phone and on-camera interviews.

There are a lot of self-help books with tips for building your confidence, wealth and health. You have heard many of these tips, including follow your passions, find balance, feel good, look good, surround yourself with positive people, eat right, do yoga, and take walks on the beach.

There is a good reason why there are so many self-help books on these topics. You must have confidence in yourself to succeed in anything really, and especially your Public Relations. If you do not like yourself (be honest here), start creating a plan to make your life better, because how you feel impacts everything—life, love, happiness, and your media interviews.

Depending on your personality and priorities, you might want to read a book by Tony Robbins (*Awaken the Giant Within*), Jack Canfield (*The Success Principles*), Tim Ferriss (*The 4-Hour Work Week*) or Barbara Corcoran (*Shark Tales*).

You can find many inspiring comeback stories about people being homeless or broke, and then becoming a successful entrepreneur. While your challenges may not be that extreme, we've all had hurdles in life.

Make it a priority for you to feel good inside. This positive energy is what is going to make you smile naturally when sharing your story in TV, radio, and print interviews.

BREATHE IN. BREATHE OUT.

Breathing in and out is also really important when you are preparing for media interviews. One of my media coaches recommended breathing exercises when I was having jitters going on TV. Before being interviewed, it really did help to take a deep breath and then let it out to calm my nerves.

Another technique that I recommend is meditation. Your meditation can be in many different formats. You may go to yoga, sit in a quiet meditative state, or simply close your eyes and visualize what you want in life.

Another way to meditate is called a walking meditation, which I do regularly in my Santa Monica beach town. Avoid talking on the phone or listening to music on your walk, and instead, just let your mind go where it wants too.

You can also do breathing exercises when walking. These breathing exercises can increase your energy, improve your mood, help you relax and inspire creativity. If you are in a hurry, breathing in and out can help calm you.

If you are not relaxed, confident, and happy inside, your anxiety will show on camera. During one of my dating advice appearances on *The Other Half*, I actually forgot the couple's name in the TV segment. My job was to give insights on whether I thought a couple, who met on an internet dating site, would make it. Forgetting their names was pretty bad. Fortunately, Mario Lopez (love him!) saved me by jumping in with the names when he saw me hesitate. Most of the audience would not even have noticed my lapse. I was forever grateful to Mario.

What no one knew was that I was working for a tech startup company at the time who surprisingly asked me to layoff some of my employees that morning. Obviously, letting employees go was very upsetting, and I carried the stress with me to this TV interview. It was really too late to cancel because the interview had been planned far in advance. We are all human, and yes, we are susceptible to unplanned twists.

You need to be ready when life throws you curve balls. Maybe if I had found more time for life balance, my delivery would have been better? I was working long hours for a very stressful startup. It was a very tough situation with no easy solution.

Along with being nervous about going on TV (which apparently is very natural), an author or expert also has to overcome feeling uneasy about speaking to large crowds. While I did thousands of training presentations early in my corporate career, it became easy with small groups. However, speaking to a really large audience was nerve wracking. When I did my breathing exercises, it was a very helpful way to get over these uncomfortable feelings.

■ Overcoming Stage Fright Example – Mega Book Marketing Conference

When I was asked to speak on stage as a testimonial in front of 700 people at *Mega Book Marketing* with Mark Victor Hansen (*Chicken Soup for the Soul* co-author) about how his conference helped me book hundreds of interviews, it was overwhelming. To calm my nerves, I used a prop. Inside the big hotel ballroom in Los Angeles, I decided to wear sunglasses on stage. With a big smile, I explained that I was grateful to be a "rock star author" with over 300 media interviews (at the time), and that they could do it too. This prop approach worked, and I grew more confident speaking to large groups.

We met so many media greats at this book marketing conference, including Mark's *Chicken Soup for the Soul* co-author Jack Canfield, bestselling author and Radio Interview Pro Alex Carroll and *New York Times* bestselling author Brendan Burchard (*Life's Golden Ticket*). We are forever grateful for what we learned there, which really launched our PR career.

Whatever you need to do to feel good inside for interviews, do it before, during, and after each opportunity.

CHAPTER 7 RECAP

When it comes to media interview showtime, this chapter is about presenting your magic clearly to reporters with confidence and conviction to maximize the response. Results may include more social media followers, increased sales or raising more money for a cause. By connecting with the audience with powerful messages, you are much more likely to achieve your media goals.

Step 7 Action Items — Hammer Home Your Interviews to Magnify Media Results

1. Practice your talking points with 8-second messaging in mind.
2. Be grateful, flexible, and early with the media.
3. Dress for success for TV interviews.
4. Speak from the heart with a genuine interest in others.
5. Speak with clarity and conviction, even if you get thrown off.
6. Be entertaining and interesting (tell me something I do not know).
7. Give real-life examples of how you helped others.
8. Smile. Breathe in. Breathe out.

PR Superpower 7 — Interview Thunder Superpower

With your Interview Thunder Superpower, you will now be able to get your point across in a way that is even more meaningful and memorable.

Chapter 7 — 8-Second PR Challenges

As we close Chapter 7, here are your *8-Second PR* Challenges:

1. What are the three to five key talking points for your story?
2. What are the top three things you need to remember when being interviewed?
3. What styles and colors make you look great on camera?
4. What can you say if you get an unexpected question from a reporter?
5. What's different about your story versus the stories of others doing similar things?
6. How are you helping others?
7. What are you doing to create balance in your life?
8. How can you relax before interviews?

Your Interview Thunder Superpower will make people want to pay more attention to you, so they stop multi-tasking and listen! By practicing these interview skills, your messages will go viral, sales will increase, and you will get invited back by the media for repeat interviews.

In the next chapter, we will talk about how to follow-up with the media and reinvent new ideas so you can keep evolving your story. Reinventing your story can literally make your brand stay in the news for years (which is why we keep talking about it)!

Follow-up and Reinvent Your Story to Extend Media Success

"You cannot use up creativity. The more you use, the more you have."

—OSCAR WILDE

A re you ready to come up with 100 ideas for different ways to pitch your story to the media? Do you like brainstorming new ways to promote your brand? We're getting to the end of this *8-Second PR* book, and your story reinvention skill is one of the most important things to master as marketer. We asked you to create ten media hooks in Chapter 4, but the reality is that you need many more for long-term Ultimate Media Success. Follow-up with new marketing campaigns, media hooks, timing, and a little luck can be your greatest assets.

Many authors and businesses make the mistake of planning a one-hit wonder promotional campaign. If a publication says "No" to a story pitch, some mistakenly think that is the end of the conversation. Instead, it is just the beginning of an ongoing dialogue. *Goody PR* pitched *Everyday Health* for over five years before scoring a media hit for *Warriors Heart* residential treatment program because we refused to give up!

If an author or product manager thinks a three-month PR product launch blitz is enough, they are sadly going to miss out on many media opportunities and sales. If you are focused only on a short-term marketing plan, that might be okay for a hobby book. However, if you are promoting a book, product, or service that is a part of a revenue-generating business or a lead generator, a three-month campaign is never enough.

For example, I was fortunate to book 53 TV interviews for *Journey Healing Centers* over four years by partnering closely with their team. This company was sold to *Elements Behavioral Health*, in 2013 who wanted to keep the brand name. This PR success story was a marathon. By regularly reinventing the "why now" story to make it relevant, along with having a genuine interest in helping others, the client became recognized as a go-to source.

> ### ■ PR Superpower 8 – Story Reinvention Superpower
>
> All brands need to continually update their media hooks to stay relevant to the latest headline news, technology and trends. To keep the interest of the media, influencers, and fans, you must master your **Story Reinvention Superpower**. This skill can help you reposition your story with new pitches—over and over and over again. Asking questions, listening, and being able to change course are powerful PR tools that are a must for repeat interviews. You cannot sustain your business or a marketing campaign by doing the same thing over and over again. To have Ultimate Media Success, you must keep the creativity going—for years—using this *8-Second PR* Superpower!

STEP 8 ACTION ITEMS — FOLLOW-UP AND REINVENT YOUR STORY TO EXTEND MEDIA SUCCESS

1. Meet the media in person to increase chances of follow-up stories.
2. Prioritize media follow-up over everything.
3. Be patient, persistent, and never desperate in your follow-up.
4. Share published stories everywhere with mentions for the outlet and reporter.
5. Measure marketing results and Calculated Publicity Value.
6. Consistently reflect on lessons learned to improve your approach.
7. Hold regular PR strategy meetings to reinvent your story.
8. Reinvent your story hooks and go back to Step 1.

PR SUPERPOWER 8 — STORY REINVENTION SUPERPOWER

The media is always looking for something different, and a good PR professional and marketing team know how to persistently reposition your story. Great PR is a continual process that requires dedication, passion and creativity. By thinking differently, you can find ways to update your Wow Story and stay in the headlines.

Let's take a closer look at these winning PR Strategies for long-term promotions.

Step 8.1 Meet the Media in Person to Increase Chances of Follow-up Stories

Whether it is a producer, host, writer, or blogger, meeting the media in person can go a long way towards building relationships and follow-up stories. If you cannot meet them, find other ways to say thank you and build a relationship!

For example, I've invested twice in the *National Publicity Summit* in New York City because it's a rare opportunity to meet reporters face-to-face and pitch story ideas. It's not cheap, but worth it to make personal connections that can be invaluable long-term.

If you cannot make it to this conference, look for other local events where reporters may speak about what they are looking for in a pitch. For example, we were fortunate to meet Jefferson Graham, who is a top technology columnist from *USA TODAY*, at a "Meet The Media" night hosted by *WeWork* in Playa Vista, California.

Once you build rapport with a reporter over the phone, you can plan to meet in person. For example, I scheduled lunch with a reporter in the Los Angeles area who writes for a national media outlet. He kept telling me that he wanted to visit *Father's Office* in my Santa Monica neighborhood for their famous hamburgers. We had a fun visit talking about his seminar ideas, newsletter, and the burger! Of course, I picked up the tab as a courtesy. While there are rules that reporters should not accept extravagant gifts from you, a hamburger, fries and a high-quality visit can go a long way. This reporter writes for a financial publication, and has quoted our clients five times in different stories.

If you are fortunate to meet IRL, be genuine and personable versus a salesperson. For our first PR client campaign, Lee Ann Del Carpio from *Rich Dad Hawaii*, we met the reporter Linda Dela Cruz from *Midweek* at a local coffee shop on Oahu. She wanted to do a profile story for the top local newspaper that had a circulation of 800,000 readers. The story was a home run for the client, who was a local business leader and consultant at the time. Ten years later, Linda is my friend on *Facebook*.

For *Warriors Heart*, we flew to San Antonio, Texas, for their Grand Opening in 2016 on their 543-acre ranch in Bandera. There were many reasons why this trip was so meaningful, including meeting the team and several local reporters in person.

We've also been fortunate to meet reporters in-studio in Los Angeles before live TV interviews for clients. In all cases, we take photos of them with the client for social media. Afterwards, we always send a sincere thank you email to producers and hosts to build long-term relationships.

Remember, most reporters are underappreciated and working at warp speed. A lunch, extra efforts to meet them, and a thank you can go a long way.

Step 8.2. Prioritize Media Follow-up over Everything

You always want to prioritize media follow-up to build your Ultimate Media Success. This follow-up may include confirming an interview and logistics, asking a question, clarifying an important point or sending a story update. The fastest way to get a new story published is through your current media relationships so stay on top of their requests.

MANAGE CURRENT INTERVIEWS

As a reminder, when a reporter emails or calls with a question about an important interview, you should drop everything and get back to them ASAP. If they are on a deadline, it is especially important, or you may lose the media opportunity.

For example, a major radio station, *710 WOR*, in New York City contacted us on a Thursday for a last-minute client interview request for that Saturday. I dropped everything to come up with the question-and-answer interview script draft. Books were also sent overnight to the host with extra copies for giveaway gifts for listeners.

MANAGE STORY UPDATES

Once a story is published by a reporter, it is best not to request any changes. Our exception to this rule is if something is inaccurate, important to fix and easy to update. Fortunately, it is much easier to ask for changes today because most stories are posted digitally. However, you always want to walk softly with reporters and only ask for small edits that are important for facts or SEO.

If a spokesperson's name or company is spelled wrong in a print publication that is already on the shelves, it will be impossible to get that fixed. However, the reporter can probably fix the online version.

Once a TV story has aired, it's impossible to fix the file once it is published online. However, if the story runs again, it may get updated. In a rare case, a client's name got fixed in a TV story banner. The segment ran on the 10:00 p.m. news, and then again the following morning at 7:00 a.m. The morning news piece had the name spelled correctly.

We are all human, and mistakes do happen. The key lesson is to ask nicely and understand the limitations reporters face when requesting edits. It is always best to send your edits in writing with "current" and "correct" lines to make an edit really easy for reporters.

And don't be afraid to keep calling back if it is an important edit. For another TV interview, we had to call a newsroom three times to get a brand name spelled correctly in the write-up. When you call, always be nice and humble by saying things such as "We know you're swamped, and would really appreciate if you would fix the name."

MANAGE FUTURE STORY REQUESTS

If a reporter says, we'd like to have you or your PR client back soon, follow-up within 24-48 hours. When we booked Tom the Tax Expert on *FOX 10 News* Phoenix, the producer explained they would like to have him back as we got closer to the tax filing deadline.

As a result, I sent the producer a follow-up email the next day with a new story hook. The first interview on March 5 was about "tips for reducing your tax filing anxiety". The second story media hook was "5 last minute tax filing tips", and it aired three weeks later in early April.

Most reporters and clients are overwhelmed, and so follow-up is a very important part of media success!

Step 8.3 Be Patient, Persistent, and Never Desperate in Your Follow-up

If you were dating, I would recommend "be patient, persistent, and never desperate," and this same advice holds true for your follow-up with reporters.

While you want to get back to them ASAP when booking interviews, there is a fine line to how much you should contact them afterwards.

Remember our *8-Second PR* Baseball Game analogy to getting a story published. Your job is to avoid getting stuck on third base doing endless follow-up because the interview is completed, but not published.

When submitting a column, it is always a gamble whether an editor will publish your story. In one case, I submitted a story for a client to an editor, and was told they did not have the staff to review it. This story was magically published ten months later without any notice. We were happy to have it show up unexpectedly in our *Google Alerts*.

In another case, I revised a story submission for a client three times based on feedback from an editor, and it was never published. Even though I spoke to the editor twice on the phone, you could tell that they were overwhelmed and on the fence about it. It was best to just let this one go.

You never know what else is pulling a producer, editor or reporter away from your story. If you think there is still a chance of coverage, don't give up until they say stop!

■ *Goody PR* Case Study - *CBS Health Watch* Win!

As an example, we worked on a *CBS Health Watch* TV interview that took about a month of back and forth follow-up. Our mantra "be patient, persistent, and never desperate" really helped while working with the producer, reporter, and client on this news segment.

We originally pitched a story idea about *Warriors Heart* Grand Opening on October 15, 2016, as the first private addiction treatment center for warriors only (military, veterans, and first responders) in the U.S. We pitched this event on October 13 and got a reply on October 16 from a producer saying they wanted to cover the story, but not the opening. This news segment eventually aired a month later on November 11 (*Veterans Day*) on over 150 *CBS TV* stations across the country, which was even better.

The time between the October 13 pitch and the November 11 story airing could be a short film about how to partner with your client and the media to produce a powerful news story. We worked closely with *Warriors Heart*, the producer in New York City and the reporter in Houston, Texas.

Fortunately, the client found great spokespeople, which included an alumni and a *Gold Star Mother*, who was also their clinical director at the time. Sadly, she lost her son to suicide after he came home from Afghanistan. Both were willing to share their stories with the world to help others.

To draft the script, we partnered with our main point person at *Warriors Heart* and the two people who volunteered to be in the story. This script draft was then sent to the *CBS Health Watch* team. Of course, these interviews did not exactly match the script, but it worked as a guideline.

For this story, a *CBS News* crew flew from Houston to San Antonio for the day to film at the *Warriors Heart* ranch on November 2. Our client preferred to have the interviews on November 1 because of a previous business trip planned, but when the *CBS News* crew was unavailable, everyone made November 2 work.

If you want to feel inspired, watch this *CBS Health Watch* story on *Warriors Heart YouTube*.

(P.S. The Calculated Publicity Value was $394,000, according to a *Nielsen* Media Report.) And yes, we sent everyone involved thank you emails and cheers.

Step 8.4 Share Published Stories Everywhere with Mentions for the Outlet and Reporter

Another way to show gratitude to reporters is to share their work all over social media. We always make posting stories a high priority and receive positive feedback often for tagging reporters and the outlet in *Facebook, Twitter, Instagram,* and *LinkedIn* posts.

Reporters will often check a spokesperson's social media following before an interview. They are counting on the interviewee to share the story once it is published with their followers. As a PR pro, I also always re-tweet, share and like a reporter's story with a mention.

For example, when *FOX 11* Los Angeles Host emailed us links to a client interview on his show "The Issue Is" on *Facebook, Twitter, Instagram* and *YouTube*, we immediately shared it everywhere on social media.

Along with sharing with our followers, we sent it to the client's book team to post on their social media. As a PR company, you should always encourage your clients to give some love to the reporter's work. They spent hours working on this earned media story. No matter how small the publication is, sharing is the least thing people can do to thank a reporter (unless you really do not like the story or feel it is inaccurate, which I have seen in very rare cases).

■ Media Multiplier Effect — *CBS 46* Atlanta Interview

You can take an interview and turn it into additional coverage through what we call the Media Multiplier Effect. For example, after the *CBS 46* Atlanta TV interview with *U.S. Air Force* Col (Ret.) Chris Stricklin about his *Warriors Heart Foundation* Awareness Campaign and Fundraiser, there were several follow-up stories.

Stricklin, who works for a consulting company called *Afterburner*, volunteered to do this PR campaign. After this TV interview, the CEO of *Afterburner*, Jim "Murph" Murphy, posted a video on *LinkedIn* congratulating Stricklin. This video and blog post not only extended this interview, but also thanked the media.

In addition, Stricklin's campaign was later highlighted in a separate *Forbes* story, and his *CBS 46* Atlanta interview was republished on ten other local TV station websites.

As a result of this media win and connection, the reporter now wants to do a follow-up story on Stricklin's company *Afterburner*. In the end, one interview turned into thirteen more stories.

There are many ways to the extend your media success. For example, you can magnify your media by posting it on a website Press page. You can also submit recaps with photographs to other outlets and reporters who cover your topic.

In addition to these ideas, PR professionals can share campaign success stories with outlets seeking case study examples. This sharing of media coverage is just another way to make one interview go viral.

Bottom line, you always want to always be brainstorming (ABB) ways to reinvent your story.

Step 8.5 Measure Marketing Results and Calculated Publicity Value

Clients are always looking for ways to measure their marketing, PR and social media results. There are many ways to calculate the value. Goals and expectations need to be set at the beginning so everyone is on the same page and to avoid misunderstandings. To provide new ideas, here are meaningful ways to measure your earned media success and ROI (Return On Investment).

■ 8 Ways to Measure Media Results

For print, radio, and TV interviews, here are eight ways to measure media success for your marketing campaigns:

1. Number of people reached (circulation, social media reach)
2. Increase in sales and customers
3. Increase in social media followers
4. Increase in website traffic
5. Donations to a cause(s)
6. Enrollments for a class or event
7. Increase in book sales and/or *Amazon* rank
8. Value of earned media (interviews) versus paid media (advertisement)

All of these media measurement categories are important for evaluating results. When we initially meet with potential clients, we always ask about their goals. These milestones contribute to an overall strategy to support the desired outcomes. Goals may include raising awareness of their brand, increasing book sales, attracting more customers, getting a column in a niche publication and/or being in a specific publication.

We also make it very clear to potential clients that if their goal is to make enough money in book sales to pay our monthly retainer fee, they are not being realistic. A book is a business card or lead-generator that usually pays very little in royalties. It important to understand that a "successful book" sells 10,000 copies. If you are making only fifty cents to one dollar for each book sale from the publisher, the earnings will probably never cover a six month minimum PR contract.

As an example, my dating book resulted in a $10,000 royalty advance from *Kensington Books*. Because you have to sell enough books to cover the advance first, I never received any more money from the publisher. Overall, *Smart Man Hunting* sold about 11,000 copies. For the international rights, I did receive another $2,300 in royalty checks from Russian and Taiwan distributors. I also made some money selling additional services, which included Internet Dating Profile Makers and Dating Coaching (not doing this anymore). However, the real return on investment did not happen until much later when I started my *Goody PR* company.

If you have a consulting business and write a book about your area of expertise, a book can be a great lead-generator for clients. This business model approach is one of the main reasons for writing this *8-Second PR* book.

■ Case Study Example - Books are Great Lead Generators

The number one way our Tax Expert client Tom Wheelwright attains clients is through people who read his *Tax-Free Wealth* book. At one point Tom discovered that he had 900 books on back-order on *Amazon*. Because this level of demand for a book is so rare unless you are a household name, his publisher asked how did this happen? The author's response was "Well, we hired a PR company!"

Of course, the backlog was a team effort, and *Goody PR* does not take full credit for this success. However, this backorder news was a GREAT PR RESULT for our client. And this client has continued to work with *Goody PR* for four years.

For media interviews, there are several things to consider when measuring earned media for print, radio, and TV stories. All of these points are important to consider when evaluating your ROI for public relations.

■ How to Measure Results for Earned Media

Measuring Print Interviews
- Number of subscribers
- Page views and visitors for the website
- Is it national or local?
- If local, what is the DMA (Designated Market Area) for the location? (Note: The DMA number indicates the nationwide rank of the media market. The number is often used by advertisers when setting paid ad rates.)
- Did the story get syndicated (picked up and shared by other outlets)?

Measuring Radio Interviews

- Number of listeners
- Is it national or local?
- If local, what is the DMA (Designated Market Area) for the market?
- Did the story get syndicated (picked up and shared by other outlets)?
- If it is a Podcast, where did it get posted (*iTunes, Stitcher, Blog Talk Radio, iHeartRadio*, etc.)
- What is the number of the station's watts?
- 10,000 watts is the minimum required for *Clear Channel* Stations.
- 50,000 watts is best because it is the highest power authorized for AM stations. The signal for a station with more watts will travel farther and reach a bigger audience.

Measuring TV Interviews

- Number of viewers
- Is it national or local?
- If local, what is the DMA (Designated Market Area) for the market?
- Did the story get syndicated (picked up and shared by other outlets)?
- What time of day did the story run?
- What would it cost to run an ad for the same length in the same timeframe?
- What is the Calculated Publicity Value? (Earned media is often worth three times paid media.)

While there are many ways to measure the success of your media, we are a huge fan of the *Nielsen* Media Reports that *Goody PR* orders with copies of TV stories. These reports show the time, audience, advertising cost, and gives a dollar value for the coverage. Sharing this information with clients is very helpful because *Nielsen* is a credible source for media data and measurement.

■ Measuring Calculated Publicity Value for TV Interviews

For the previously mentioned *KTLA Channel 5* Los Angeles book launch interview, the length was 5.5 minutes. The Calculated Publicity Value, according to a *Nielsen* Media Report, was over $46,000 because of the length and major market.

Los Angeles is the #2 DMA (Designated Marketing Area) in the country behind New York City. DMAs are used for advertising rates. The #2 DMA rank impacted the Calculated Publicity Value* for this *KTLA* interview.

It is very important to understand different ways to show your clients how to measure success. Another way to explain the ROI is that your earned media is worth 3x the value as paid media. In this case, if you bought ads for the same amount of time, the estimate is that it would cost $15,540. If we multiply it x3, the Calculated Publicity Value = $46,620.

Social media marketing measurements are a completely different story. It is about exposure, engagement and Calls to Action. I could write a whole book about the strategies for valuing fan engagements.

■ *8-Second PR* Digital Marketing Class for Authors

Based on feedback from authors and experts, we will offer an *8-Second PR* Digital Marketing Class for Authors starting in 2019. Visit GoodyPR. com or our book website 8SecondPR.com for more information.

If you are not getting the desired results from your marketing campaigns, it is time to brainstorm new ideas. To reposition the brand story, consider a different spokesperson, schedule a special event and/or do a fundraiser for your charity. It is hard to predict what will click with the media. Keep reminding yourself over and over again to "Never Give Up". You can go for a walk, do A/B testing on social media, ask for input at your favorite local coffee shop and/or hire a PR professional or agency.

Step 8.6 Consistently Reflect on Lessons Learned to Improve Your Approach

One of the best things that Robert Kiyosaki (*Rich Dad Poor Dad*) teaches entrepreneurs and small business owners is never fear failure. Instead, many say that you should embrace failures by reflecting on the lessons learned. Mistakes can actually make a business even stronger. We can all get better in anything we do by failing forward.

Marketing is all about testing story ideas to see what connects best to customers to get the desired result. For our company name, it was changed from *Sunrise Road Media* to *Goody PR* in 2014 after the *Goody Awards* for social good became so popular. People were so confused by *Sunrise Road Media* because it was too broad. There was no "wow factor" and it took us way too long to explain it. When changed it to *Goody PR* with a "…" to represent our multiple services, including marketing, PR, and social media marketing, it was a great solution.

Originally, I came up with *Sunrise Road Media* in Hawaii while working on our first integrated marketing campaign for *Rich Woman*. While the sunrises on Kailua Beach were magnificent, I had to be honest and admit that my business name was not working.

Once we changed the name to *Goody PR*, our clients and referrals doubled within a year. Your brand name really does matter. If your story is not connecting with customers and the media, take a hard look in the mirror, ask for honest feedback, and make changes.

In addition to lessons learned about your brand, you have to look at PR campaigns honestly to see what worked versus flopped. Sometimes it is as simple as adding a level of urgency to your pitch email subject line to get more media coverage. Other times, you have to switch gears completely with new media hooks.

Using *Constant Contact* is a great way to test story ideas via email because it tells you what percent of reporters actually opened the pitch email.

In some cases, our first email resulted in immediate interview requests such as *The Howard Stern Wrap Up Show* for Danny Zuker's new book. In this case, I sent a personalized email to the right contact. Because Danny got his start there as an intern a long time ago, it was an easier sell.

In other cases, it is harder to understand what works best. A pitch with a sense of urgency in it or a local expert usually gets more hits.

■ *Goody PR* Case Studies – Pitch Email Open Rates

July 2 Email (resulted in TV interview)

Pitch – 4th of July – How Making Flags is Healing Veterans and First Responders

Local TV Reporters – 50% Open Rate

July 2 Email

Pitch – 4th of July – How Making Flags is Healing Veterans and First Responders

National Reporters – 14% Open Rate

June 30 Email

Pitch –TODAY– Liberty Day Festival with *U.S. Air Force* (ret) Col Chris Sticklin Mission

Local TV Reporters – 50% Open Rate

In the June 30 example above, the local Birmingham TV stations did not cover this Liberty Day Festival. However, I received an email reply from a local *CBS News* reporter a month prior showing interest in this *Warriors Heart Foundation* Fundraiser. She did not get the story approved originally, and so we kept sending this producer new versions of the story. On July 3, this producer finally got the green light to do a profile piece connected to the *Fourth of July* holiday and the flags made by veterans and first responders at *Warriors Heart*. The story was a result of the continual follow-up, and constantly reinventing the media hook. The spokesperson, *U.S. Air Force* Col (ret) Chris Stricklin, was also a great PR partner in this case.

Step 8.7 Hold Regular PR Strategy Meetings to Reinvent Your Story

As we have discussed, marketing campaigns should be an ongoing process with different initiatives that go beyond a three-month PR blitz. The company, product, service, book, and/or the expert spokesperson can continually benefit from promotions that are regularly updated.

For example, we meet monthly with *Goody PR* clients to have a formal strategy meeting with report summaries. While we are constantly brainstorming new ideas for media hooks and opportunities, this scheduled meeting includes a formal agenda, suggestions, and action item notes.

During these PR strategy meetings, we discuss the status of current projects, media interviews, press releases, upcoming new projects, books, what's in the news that may be relevant, and then develop a plan for the next month and beyond. Each client's strategy is ever-changing, depending on the business priorities, breaking news, and feedback.

The first few months with a new client are probably the most important for getting your story straight. To illustrate this point, here's a case study that we love:

■ *Goody PR* Case Study — Book Brand Story Repositioning

When *Goody PR* client @ Danny Zuker launched the pre-order version of his new book, *He Started It!: My Twitter War with Trump* (September 2018), we got early feedback from reviewers that showed people expected a novel length book versus a packaged 94-page *Twitter* exchange with commentary.

Many librarians who asked for preview copies did not understand *Twitter*, and we discovered quickly that we were attracting the wrong audience. As a result, the book team brainstormed how to clarify this new product better.

To make the book mission and format more clear, the social media manager, Liz Dubelman, recommended saying, "This is a short, powerful, and unconventional book to support charity." As a result, we repositioned the book as a "gift item" where 100% of the author profits went to three charities, including *Planned Parenthood, World Wildlife Fund,* and *RAICES (Refugee and Immigration Center for Education and Legal Services).*

To make the book even more meaningful, I recommended adding voters to the dedication and launch a *Rock the Vote* campaign. Then, the editor Paul Slansky added people who get their friends to vote and the free press to the dedication. These updates were added to the original dedication to women victimized. All changes came from the heart and better represented the author's goals to make a positive impact with his book.

This repositioning exercise made the book more relevant to current events with the 2018 Midterm Elections just weeks away, and was more aligned with the author's intentions. The PR campaign then became a *Rock the Vote* initiative with a much bigger story.

As a result of making these brand story updates, media placements included *CNN, TMZ Live, The Howard Stern Wrap-Up Show, The Adam Carolla Show* (one of the biggest podcasts in the world), *Chicago Tribune, Los Angeles Times, Dr. Drew Midday Live with Lauren Sivan, Good Day LA, AXS,* bloggers, and more.

Your story reinvention process should never end if you want to stay in business! This creative process is what can continually energize your story. It is fun for me, and why I love magnifying good. If you like this brainstorming process, too, you just read the right book.

Step 8.8 Reinvent Your Story Hooks and Go Back to Step 1

Do you have new ideas ready to attract more media now? The overall theme throughout this chapter (and really this book) has been the power of reinventing your story so more people are talking about your brand.

The *8-Second PR* process is actually a lot like writing a book. The first draft is horrible, and then, you re-write it three to ten times to shape a compelling story with a strong "wow factor." If you like doing this exercise over and over again, marketing can be a great career. It may feel like *Groundhog Day*, and your job is to prevent fans and media from getting bored by giving a new meaning to your brand story.

For *Goody PR*'s small business and brand expert clients, we have worked with several CEOs and founders for years on a monthly retainer. We prefer these long-term clients because we LOVE being part of their team. As a PR partner, we continually revise their message and media outreach strategies. It is also more powerful to be part of an overall business plan and see the long-term results.

Goody PR is constantly brainstorming ways to enhance the story for these VIP clients, along with ways to improve their overall business.

■ *Goody PR* **Case Study - Rock the Vote Campaign for Book Launch**

When *Goody PR* recommended a #RockTheVote Campaign to promote *Modern Family* EP Danny Zuker's new book, *He Started It! My Twitter War with Trump* (September 2018), the 2018 Midterm Elections were just three months away. With the book now dedicated to voters, we worked with Zuker's team to add more elements to the campaign.

Charitybuzz Auction for Charity - We learned that this platform is like an *eBay* for charity. You post an item, people bid for two weeks, and the highest bidder wins. For this client, we set up an auction to benefit *Planned Parenthood* (one of the charities supported by the book). The prize was a *Modern Family* LA set tour, an autographed script

---

written and signed by the *Emmy* Winner and the cast, along with four autographed books. The winning bid was $2,750.00, which was split 80/20 between the designated charity and *Charitybuzz*.

Digital Hollywood Producers Panel and Book Table – Because the author is a successful TV executive and writer, we pitched Zuker as a panelist and organized a book table at the happy hour at this digital media conference. We got the green light for both, and there were about 150 people who attended the panel.

#RockTheVote Book Talk and Signing – To reach more digital influencers, we worked with the *Social Media Club Los Angeles* to host a special #RockTheVote book talk and signing two weeks before the election. Our team asked *What's Tending* co-founder Shira Lazar to be the MC and interview author Danny Zuker and editor and political satirist Paul Slansky. This event really went way beyond the original scope of the PR contract. However, I am a member of the *Social Media Club Los Angeles* (SMCLA) Board. The board agreed to proceed if I would manage everything (securing the venue, overall organization, communications, and event sponsors). In the end, the book team and *SMCLA* rallied, and the event was a big success for everyone.

Pop Culture and Politics Media Hook – Because Zuker's current tweets about breaking news were regularly quoted in media stories, we repositioned him as a "Twitter Historian" who could weigh in on how pop culture and politics were colliding.

All of these initiatives resulted in more media stories, including an invitation back to *CNN*, two more interviews on *FOX 11*, and a *KTLA Channel 5 Morning News* story solely about his *Rock The Vote* Campaign. These results show the power of revising a media hook and story!

Because we are close to the end of this book, here's a quick recap of eight ways to reinvent a story for your Ultimate Media Success!

■ 8 Ways to Make Your Story Relevant

1. Connect the story to a major news headline.
2. Connect your story to a season (summer, fall, winter, or spring).
3. Connect your story to a time of year for your business (examples: tax season for tax experts and spring buying season for real estate experts.)

4. Connect your story to a holiday (there are so many holidays now, so always include references to back-up your pitch if it is not a highly recognized holiday.)
5. Connect your story to a major event (Examples: awards, movie premiere, elections).
6. Connect your story to a celebrity (ask a celebrity to tweet about it).
7. Connect your story to a charity (all *Goody PR* clients must have a charity).
8. Connect your story to pop culture events (movies, concerts, what's trending).

CHAPTER 8 RECAP

When it comes to reinventing your story, this process should be something that you embrace every day.

Step 8 Action Items — Follow-up and Reinvent Your Story to Extend Media Success

1. Meet the media in person to increase chances of follow-up stories.
2. Prioritize media follow-up questions over everything.
3. Be patient, persistent, and never desperate in your follow-up.
4. Share published stories everywhere with mentions for the outlet and reporter.
5. Measure marketing results and Calculated Publicity Value.
6. Consistently reflect on lessons learned to improve your approach.
7. Hold regular PR strategy meetings to reinvent your story.
8. Reinvent your story hooks and go back to Step 1.

PR Superpower 8 — Story Reinvention Superpower

With your new Story Reinvention Superpower, you will now be able to get your point across in a way that is meaningful, relevant and memorable.

Chapter 8 — 8-Second PR Challenges

As we close Chapter 8, here are your *8-Second PR* Challenges:

1. How are you going to meet and thank the media?
2. How often are you going to follow-up with print, radio, and TV reporters about when a story will be published?
3. How can you help your media interviews go viral by sharing and repurposing them?
4. How are you going to measure results for your media interviews for your clients?
5. How often are you going to launch new marketing campaigns?
6. How often are you going to hold strategy meetings?
7. When do you know that it is time to reinvent the story?
8. Are you still having fun?

Your Story Reinvention Superpower will help you expand media opportunities for brands for months and years.

In the Conclusion, I will recap all of the eight PR Superpowers that you have learned in this book, along with suggesting ways to celebrate your wins! Every interview is a WIN, and it is important to give yourself cheers along this journey!

Conclusion

"Create your own style...Let it be unique for yourself and yet identifiable for others."

—DAME ANNA WINTOUR, EDITOR IN CHIEF, VOGUE

Now that you have a new set of *8-Second PR* tools, a WOW Story and eight PR Superpowers, let's wrap this book up with some encouraging words, next steps and a roadmap for your Ultimate Media Success.

By now you know that getting an interview published is not easy. Every time you get an earned media hit through traditional PR (print, radio, or TV) or digital PR (blog, video, photographs, and social media) with stories that shine a positive light on your brand, celebrate your win!

Remember, you are playing *8-Second PR* Baseball, and your job is to continually advance your story versus get stuck on third base with never-ending interview follow-ups! If you score an earned media hit that promotes you and your work, share it in a humble way with the world!

As long as your content continues to entertain and educate your audience, your fans and media will keep coming back for more. Your company and book are not going away. Your challenge is to keep sending out new pitches, book continual media coverage and make a positive impact.

I will forever be grateful to the people who helped make my first media hits happen. From the two PR companies whom I hired to the reporters, producers, editors, family, friends, and fans, I cannot thank you enough for your support.

Remember, PR is a team sport, and you cannot do it alone.

If you are just getting your PR process started, these first wins are meant to inspire you to keep moving forward. Every positive story is a major milestone, and I wish you the same success in your area of expertise.

CELEBRATE YOUR FIRSTS!

Major PR Milestone	What happened?
First Major Magazine Story – *Cosmopolitan*	I remember being in *Cosmopolitan Magazine* with a sidebar story, which was perfect for my dating book audience. It listed seven of my tips and referenced my full name and book title. I later went to visit the Hearst building in NYC and was able to thank some of the reporters in person.
First National Newspaper Story – *USA TODAY*	When I was mentioned by *USA TODAY* for the first time, I was on pins and needles the night before the story was scheduled to be published. The reporter told me that if there was breaking news, it might get cut and there were no guarantees. I asked my father on the East Coast (I was in Los Angeles) to buy the paper and call me at 6:00 a.m. PST if I made it into the story. When my father called, he was so excited. Not only was I quoted, but there was a sidebar story highlighting my tips!
First Local TV Interview – ABC2 WMAR-TV Baltimore	For my first local TV news interview, I am grateful to a high school friend named Dabney who helped me book it. I was in a complete zone and can barely remember it. My parents were so excited that they played it repeatedly during a special book signing at their house that weekend. I remember being SO embarrassed by what I looked like on TV with anchor Jamie Costello, but was so grateful for the support of my family and hometown! We sold over 100 books at this book signing.
First National TV Talk Show Interview - *The Other Half*	For my first national TV talk show interview on *The Other Half* (guys' version of *The View*), I was fortunate to be on a panel as the dating expert with Hollywood legend Dick Clark, Danny Bonaduce (*The Partridge Family*), and Mario Lopez (*EXTRA*), along with Gretchen Frazier, who was seeking relationship advice. I met Gretchen while getting makeup touch-ups. Yes, I was nervous and barely remember it. Afterwards, I became friends with Gretchen and was happy to attend her wedding to a different guy a few years later.

Major PR Milestone	What happened?
First National TV News Interview in NYC – *FOX News National*	For my first national TV news interview in New York, I was SO grateful to have my friend connect me with *FOX News* entertainment reporter Bill McCuddy. Not only did screenwriter and comedian Dan Rosen help me secure this interview, but he gave great advice on the script and jokes! My book was on the *Amazon* bestseller list for a week after that interview. One of the best results was getting on the producer's "dating expert list", which resulted in several follow-up interviews!
First Radio Interviews – *RTIR*	I will always be grateful to *RTIR (Radio-Television Interview Report)* for their promotional magazine that is sent to over 4,000 radio producers around the country. I used *RTIR* to promote all three versions of my dating book with half-page ads (now online only). I also attended their *National Publicity Summit* in New York City. The result was over 150 radio interviews! Thank you Bill and Steve Harrison.
First Paid Column – *Smart Woman*	I am also grateful for my first paid column published in *Smart Woman* magazine in Baltimore, Maryland, by editor Sabina Dana Plasse. It is always best to start PR in your hometown. Baltimore has been very kind to me as an author. All of the local TV stations had me as a guest during my five years of promotion.
First National Column – *Yahoo!*	After writing for smaller blogs, we were so honored to receive our first national column with *Yahoo!* The editor Rad Dewey is now our friend on *Facebook* fifteen years later. To build this relationship, we actually went to the *Yahoo!* Headquarters in Sunnyvale, California, to meet Rad and his team in person. We wore our *Yahoo!* baseball hat for years after this lunch.

You can also achieve all of these media milestones and success while promoting a personal or business brand. I have received no reply or been told "No" many more times than "Yes". The key is to "be patient, persistent and never desperate." Of course it also helped to brainstorm with friends how to reach these contacts and get referrals. You can do this too! Look for the PR opportunities, and make them happen!

So let's review what you've learned in this book as an *8-Second PR* Roadmap to your Ultimate Media Success. It's a lot of information to digest, and it's ok to be overwhelmed. You will increase your confidence and results as you fine-tune your PR process. You have the information and PR Superpowers to see through obstacles. You can do this!

■ 8 Ultimate Media Success Goals

As an example, here are eight Ultimate Media Success Goals for PR that should be customized by each individual, brand, or marketing professional. Dig deep and define what you aim to achieve from your PR. Once achieved, each of these milestones should be considered big wins:

1. Get monthly interviews published.
2. Increase book sales and/or clients.
3. Increase email subscribers.
4. Increase social media followers.
5. Increase brand awareness.
6. Raise funds for a charity.
7. Make a difference.
8. Attract a speakers agent.

If you achieve all of your desired results, it's time for a major celebration with your team and/or clients. The combination of the *8-Second PR* Superpowers can turn these goals into reality with bottom line results. And remember, one media story can literally reach millions of potential clients and fans.

It's the combination of your results and eight new *8-Second PR* Superpowers that will get you to your Ultimate Media Success. Together, these strengths can result in hundreds of media hits for your brand.

To make your story unstoppable, use your new *8-Second PR* Superpowers and process. Go back to the eight steps in this book when needed for examples and suggestions. You can also help others magnify their good by sharing this book with friends who want to break through noise in their niche online.

Liz H. Kelly

■ *8-Second PR* Story Energizer Process

1. Define Your Wow Story to Inspire Fans and Media.
2. Dominate Your Digital Bank to Increase Word-of-Mouth Marketing.
3. Write Compelling Content with Unlimited Strength to Move Readers.
4. Write Powerful Media Hooks to Connect with Reporters.
5. Target Your Audience with Media Vision to Laser Focus.
6. Make Your Interview Take Flight to Score Mega Media.
7. Hammer Home Your Interviews to Magnify Media Results.
8. Follow-up and Reinvent Your Story to Extend Media Success.

It will take time and practice, but you can get your brand in your ideal media to reach the right audience! I am still learning and continue to seek advice from other PR professionals.

The most important thing is not to never give up when promoting a story, especially if it is your true passion! Even if you are told "No" hundreds of times, commit to keep going.

With your new *8-Second PR* Superpowers, you will energize your story with continual earned media!

■ *8-Second PR* Superpowers = Ultimate Media Success

1. WOW Storytelling Superpower
2. Digital PR Superpower
3. Unlimited Content Strength Superpower
4. Media Hook Superpower
5. Media Vision Superpower
6. Interview Flight Superpower
7. Interview Thunder Superpower
8. Story Reinvention Superpower

As a quick reference, keep your new *8-Second PR* Process and Superpowers nearby to encourage you to continue moving forward.

While this *8-Second PR* Roadmap Summary can be overwhelming, it's important to make a plan and commit to working on one-two action items per day, and you will finish in about two months. Use whatever organization tool works best for you (*Excel, Notes, Evernote, Calendar Reminders, Outlook*) to get these items on your radar.

8-SECOND PR ROADMAP SUMMARY

Step 1 – Define Your Wow Story to Inspire Fans and Media

■ PR Superpower 1 - Wow Storytelling Superpower

We want you to go way beyond telling a great brand story using the **Wow Storytelling Superpower**. By mastering your message, you can inspire fans, media and influencers to make your story go viral. You want to make a lasting impression that moves the reader, reporter, or customer to share your brand story over and over again. Yes, you want to find an A-team, unique product, and powerful spokespeople, but ultimately, your media results go back to the story. If you have the determination and dedication to edit your story more than 100 times to make it truly inspiring, you will have Ultimate Media Success. You've got this with your first *8-Second PR* Superpower.

For Chapter 1, here are your *8-Second PR* Challenges:

1. How can you get someone's attention in eight seconds?
2. How can you tell your brand story in one to two sentences?
3. What were 3 game changers in your life that led you to your ideal job?
4. What work would you do for free?
5. What are three things that describe your brand in one sentence?
6. Can you share a mission statement with a powerful meaning in eight seconds?
7. What are your three to seven key selling points?
8. When are you going to schedule time to work on enhancing your Wow Story?

Step 2 – Dominate Your Digital Bank to Increase Word-of-Mouth Marketing

■ PR Superpower 2 – Digital PR Superpower

Once you have a brand name idea, the next thing you want to do is dominate your digital bank. For Ultimate Media Success, you must enhance your **Digital PR Superpower** to increase your Word-of-Mouth Marketing. You want to own your digital assets with the same superhuman strength as a superhero. Your digital bank includes a dot com URL, mobile-friendly websites, social media channels, blog names, videos, photographs, graphics, and more. If you embrace digital marketing, your content will be listed all over the first page of *Google* results when someone searches on your product's name. To get everyone talking about your brand, you must master this *8-Second PR* Superpower!

For Chapter 2, here are your *8-Second PR* Challenges:

1. Are you able to secure your exact match .com and top three social media usernames for your brand?
2. What is your SEO (Search Engine Optimization) keyword strategy for your content?
3. How is your website content going to wow a fan in eight seconds?
4. What is your visual marketing strategy for photos to tell a story in eight seconds?
5. What are you going to include in the first eight seconds of your videos to engage your audience?
6. What is your 2-3 minute brand story video going to include?
7. Can you tell a powerful story in a tweet that is clear, concise and compelling?
8. What marketing elements will be in one of your digital marketing campaigns?

Step 3 - Write Compelling Content with Unlimited Strength to Move Readers

■ PR Superpower 3 – Unlimited Strength Content Superpower

Once you own your digital domain, it is time to magnify your brand story with clear, concise, and compelling content that will stand the test of time. To move readers, use the **Unlimited Strength Content Superpower** to write moving content that is unstoppable. You can gain the undivided attention of your fans by creating press releases, columns, blogs, videos, and social media posts with timely, relevant, and/or "evergreen" content. An evergreen story is a plus because it has a long shelf-life and remains fresh for years to your target market audience. Evergreen story examples include annual recaps, interviews, how-to guides, case studies, product reviews, lists (top tips), best practices, and success stories. Get ready to dig deeper into how to build lasting impressions using this *8-Second PR* Superpower.

For Chapter 3, here are your *8-Second PR* Challenges:

1. What are five compelling announcements and headlines you can write in eight words or less about your brand, product, or service?
2. What are 3 evergreen stories that you can pitch?
3. How will the first sentence for each piece of content compel the reader to continue?
4. Whom can you quote to add value to the content?
5. What statistics can add strength to your story?
6. What is the high-level outline for your content?
7. Are you going to send out press releases, and which service will you use?
8. Who is going to proofread your content and/or provide feedback?

Step 4 - Write Powerful Media Hooks to Connect with Reporters

> **■ PR Superpower 4 – Media Hook Superpower**
>
> To help your brand get more earned media (where someone else shares your story through TV, radio, print or digital), use the **Media Hook Superpower**. You always want to pitch a powerful media hook to make your ideas resonate with the reporter. With an eight-second adult attention span, you need to immediately grab the reporter's interest in your email subject line, pitch headline and/or first sentence. Once you have sold the right reporter on your story idea, their media coverage can give your brand way more credibility than any paid advertisement. If you build a good relationship with the reporter and have a reputation that you are "easy to work with and provide great content," they will keep coming back for more. Use these story pitching tips and *8-Second PR* Superpower to make lasting impressions, and extend your long-term Ultimate Media Success!

For Chapter 4, here are your *8-Second PR* Challenges:

1. What are three compelling media hooks for each of your clients/projects?
2. What will you write in your email subject line to get a reporter to open it?
3. How will the first sentence in your email or phone pitch grab their attention?
4. Who will be your spokesperson—and do they have a moving story?

5. How is your spokesperson/expert or organization positively impacting lives?
6. Does your story pitch include testimonials from your client's customers, and are they willing to speak on camera about it?
7. What type of visuals can you provide to illustrate your media hook?
8. How are you going to use social media to research timely topics and trends?

Step 5 - Target Your Audience with Media Vision to Laser Focus

> **■ PR Superpower 5 – Media Vision Superpower**
>
> You want to use your **Media Vision Superpower** to connect with the right contact who is genuinely interested in your story. To reach your ideal media, fans, and influencers, laser focus your research to see through obstacles. To enhance this PR superpower, *Google* to find out what your preferred reporters and media outlets are talking about online. Sure, most people would like to be in *USA TODAY* or on *CNN*. However, media placements do not happen magically just because you asked a reporter at a news outlet. You need to pitch the right media hook to the right person at the right time, just to have a chance of your story being published to the public. It is critical to fine-tune this *8-Second PR* Superpower to achieve your PR goals.

For Chapter 5, here are your *8-Second PR* Challenges:

1. Who is your ideal target market for customers and media? Consider interests, income, geography, and more.
2. What three publications are on the top of your media outlet wish list?
3. If you do PR, who are the top three preferred reporters for each client?
4. How can you build long-term relationships with your preferred media?
5. Who are key influencers for your client's product or service?
6. How can you build long-term relationships with key influencers in your areas of expertise?
7. What are five different ways to pitch the same thing?
8. What days and times are you going to try pitching?

Step 6 - Make Your Interview Take Flight to Score Mega Media

■ PR Superpower 6 – Interview Flight Superpower

Many authors and experts do not realize that just because you get an interview request, it does not mean a story will be published. Your **Interview Flight Superpower** can help you follow-up consistently to score mega media hits! When you receive an interview request from a reporter, you're up at bat. However, even if they do the interview, it might not be shared. Like scoring a run in baseball, getting in the headlines is a process that takes skill, endurance, and patience! Every time you get a media opportunity, you want to be prepared to advance the story around the bases until it crosses home plate as a published story! If you stumble, get back up again until you score earned media using this *8-Second PR* Superpower!

For Chapter 6, here are your *8-Second PR* Challenges:

1. What tools can you set up to help you reply to a reporter within one hour of an interview request?
2. What are you going to include in an electronic press kit?
3. How are you going to set expectations with your clients so they can help you reply to media requests with warp speed?
4. What Q-and-A scripts do you have ready for your clients to send TV producers?
5. How often are you going to follow-up with the media if your story does not get around the bases and score?
6. When do you know it's time to give up on the story follow-up?
7. How can you show your appreciation and support for a story on social media?
8. How are you going to thank reporters after a story is published?

Step 7 - Hammer Home Your Interviews to Magnify Media Results

■ PR Superpower 7 – Interview Thunder Superpower

Messaging is a PR art that you can master with the **Interview Thunder Superpower**. When you get the opportunity to do an interview with a reporter, make sure to be GRATEFUL first and then be prepared to hammer home your messages. For TV, print, radio and podcasts, you want to move your audience with powerful soundbites. Use emphasis statements and examples of how you have helped others to quickly draw attention to your story. Just as thunder can make you stop what you are doing and look up, you want people to stop multi-tasking and focus on what you are saying. Your thunder will be impacted by your ability to deliver great content with a memorable delivery. For TV, your tone of voice, non-verbal expressions, props, and what you wear all matter in a very visual world. If you speak with confidence and conviction from the heart, you will make lasting impressions using this *8-Second PR* Superpower!

For Chapter 7, here are your *8-Second PR* Challenges:

1. What are the three to five key talking points for your story?
2. What are the top three things you need to remember when being interviewed?
3. What styles and colors make you look great on camera?
4. What can you say if you get an unexpected question from a reporter?
5. What's different about your story versus the stories of others doing similar things?
6. How are you helping others?
7. What are you doing to create balance in your life?
8. How can you relax before interviews?

Step 8 - Follow-up and Reinvent Your Story to Extend Media Success

■ PR Superpower 8 – Story Reinvention Superpower

All brands need to continually update their media hooks to stay relevant to the latest headline news, technology and trends. To keep the interest of the media, influencers, and fans, you must master your **Story Reinvention Superpower**. This skill can help you reposition your story with new pitches—over and over and over again. Asking questions, listening, and being able to change course are powerful PR tools that are a must for repeat interviews. You cannot sustain your business or a marketing campaign by doing the same thing over and over again. To have Ultimate Media Success, you must keep the creativity going—for years—using this *8-Second PR* Superpower!

Liz H. Kelly

For Chapter 8, here are your *8-Second PR* Challenges:

1. How are you going to meet and thank the media?
2. How often are you going to follow-up with print, radio, and TV reporters about when a story will be published?
3. How can you help your media interviews go viral by sharing and repurposing them?
4. How are you going to measure results for your media interviews for your clients?
5. How often are you going to launch new marketing campaigns?
6. How often are you going to hold strategy meetings?
7. When do you know that it is time to reinvent the story?
8. Are you still having fun?

Are you now ready for your Ultimate Media Success?

You've got this! You have all the PR Superpowers you need.

Do not overthink this. Make a plan, and start learning from the process!

Remember, it's a PR Marathon versus a sprint.

Just start.

The end. (Well, not really, it is just the beginning of your story).

■ *8-SECOND PR* Request - BOOK REVIEWS

If you found this *8-Second PR* book helpful, we would be very grateful if you post a book review on *Amazon*. Feedback is a "gift," and your thoughts on what was most helpful (or not) can provide insights on what to pitch to the media!

If you post a review for our book, please tweet it and include @ LizHKelly so we get a notice. We will be happy to follow you back on *Twitter* and tweet about your book if you are an author.

Acknowledgements

Thank you, Mom, for your writing skills, encouragement, and quirky sense of humor!

Thank you, Dad, for being president of my first book's fan club, endless LOLs, and teaching us storytelling skills!

Thank you to our *Goody PR* Clients for your partnership, ideas, and gratitude over the past ten years. Your stories have inspired us to continue magnifying good!

Thank you to my first PR teams and media coaches who got me started on the right track, especially Jess Todtfeld, Jamie Feldstein, and Roberta Gale.

Thank you, Vicki Winters, for finding my first literary agent and for being SUCH a passionate cheerleader!

Thank you, Jane Turner, for getting me to write a journal again. It was very healing, and got us to write again.

Thank you to every reporter who ever answered my call, responded to an email pitch, and interviewed me or one of our clients!

Thank you to PR pros who have been sounding boards and advisors over the past fifteen years, especially Ann Flower, Evelyn Jerome Alexander, and Bill Harrison.

Thank you to Lee Ann Del Carpio for being our first ever client. Sending you aloha love!

Special thanks to Lisa and Josh Lannon for being our PR partner on this journey as a VIP client during the past decade for *Warriors Heart* and *Journey Healing Centers*. Your businesses, financial education, philanthropic contributions and book (*The Social Capitalist*) continue to inspire us and millions around the world!

Thank you Former Special Forces and *Warriors Heart* Co-Founder Tom Spooner and *US Air Force* Col (ret) Chris Stricklin for your many sacrifices protecting our freedom.

Thank you, Tom Wheelwright and your *WealthAbility* team (Clarissa, Clint, Irene and Ann). It's been a true honor to constantly brainstorm your story and continually promote your educational products and services. Your enthusiasm and passion are contagious!

Special shout out to everyone on Danny Zuker's book team, including Liz Dubelman, Paul Slansky and Dan Vallancourt. It was an honor to work with each of you for so many reasons!

Thank you to my rock star book team Yvette Bowlin, Bader Howar (Bader Howar Photography), Heidi North (book cover), Meriam Bouarrouji, mom and Narinder.

And many thanks to our family and friends (you know who you are!) for listening, being there, and providing cheers throughout this marketing journey. We could not write this book and magnify good without your support.

Resources

Because the focus of *8-Second PR* has been primarily on brand storytelling, here are a few recommended resources, tools, and reading for you. Please visit our GoodyPR.com website for more tips, tools and our *8-Second PR* Digital Marketing Class for Authors.

Media Outreach Resources

Cision – National database of reporters (access to 300,000 members for annual fee)

Haro (Help A Reporter Out) – Press Queries posted by reporters

RTIR – Radio Television Interview Report

Email Marketing Resources

Constant Contact

Mailchimp

Press Releases

PR Newswire – most expensive and biggest reach

Business Wire

Marketing Wire

PR Web

Digital Marketing Tips Reading

Mashable

Social Media Examiner

Social Media Club Los Angeles

Social Media Management Resources

Hootsuite

Sprout Social

Hubspot

Buffer

Tailwind (Instagram post scheduling)

Photo Apps

Adobe PhotoShop Mix

Live Collage

Camera+

Books

Media Secrets: A Media Training Crash Course (2016) by Jess Todtfeld

---

■ Goody PR . . . Marketing, PR, and Social Media Marketing Services

If you do not have time to do everything in this book, please contact us at info@goodypr.com to discuss ways you may want to hire our team. Check out our Services page with a menu of ways we may be able to work with you: goodypr.com/Services

---

Client Testimonials

Kelly's PR efforts and innovative ideas have been an integral part of our marketing team's success for the past four years. After booking hundreds of media interviews, we had 900 Tax-Free Wealth books on backorder on Amazon. When our publisher asked, what did you do, we said, well we hired a publicist. If you're looking for a great PR partner to promote your business, I highly recommend Liz Kelly.

—TOM WHEELWRIGHT, CPA, CEO OF WEALTHABILITY AND
TAX-FREE WEALTH AUTHOR

Liz Kelly partnered with our Journey Healing Centers team on the Public Relations for 4 years, which included writing monthly press releases, pitching to the media, booking interviews, media coaching, and editing contributing writer stories. Her work contributed to our increased brand awareness, 53 TV interviews and educating the public. Liz was also on top of breaking news stories, and was willing to always work no matter the day or time when we got interview requests. She has tremendous follow through and keeps on top of what is going on. I highly recommend Liz and Goody PR.

—LISA LANNON, AUTHOR, SOCIAL ENTREPRENEUR,
AND *RICH DAD ADVISOR*

Liz Kelly's enthusiasm, creativity and teamwork approach all contributed to a PR campaign that went way beyond the goals set for my book launch. With over 40 media hits (interviews and syndicated stories), two speaking events and a Charitybuzz campaign for one of our book charities in 3 months, it was off the charts. If you want a PR pro who knows how to adapt and adjust to headline news to amplify your story, I highly recommend Goody PR and Liz Kelly.

—DANNY ZUKER, *MODERN FAMILY* EXECUTIVE PRODUCER, 5-TIME EMMY WINNER AND AUTHOR, HE STARTED IT!: MY TWITTER WAR WITH TRUMP

We were lucky to be one of Goody PR's 5 VIP clients during this past year that made us look like pros in launching Autism Guardian Angels (AGA). Goody PR partnered with us to develop a brand story, mission, logo, custom website, compelling content and an integrated marketing campaign for Autism Awareness Month that put us on the map with peer recognition and media within a month. We're grateful for all their hard work and dedication to creating a fun AGA brand that matched our mission to "bring out the brilliance in exceptional children and adults with autism by investing in tools that increase their smiles, confidence and independence".

—DAVID LUBER, *AUTISM GUARDIAN ANGELS* AND LCC PROPERTIES GROUP FOUNDER

Thank you Liz H Kelly and Goody PR for pushing our DGA Memorial Day Premiere forward with marketing, PR, social media and sponsorships at the last minute. Within 10 days, it was amazing that you secured 2 news segments on KCBS and KTLA, food sponsors that made dinner for the Marines from Camp Pendleton possible, 2 photographers, special Golden Goody Award for WWII veteran Leon Cooper, videos and social media marketing support. Your marketing campaign blitz has greatly contributed to Vanilla Fire Productions being in negotiations for funding a sequel, only one week after this event! We can't thank you enough!

—STEVEN C BARBER, *VANILLA FIRE PRODUCTIONS* CO-FOUNDER & EXECUTIVE PRODUCER

It was great to bring Liz back for a second social media training workshop at The Recording Academy (GRAMMYs) for local members and clients of MusiCares. There was a lot of positive attendee feedback for her 2.0 class held June 2013 which focused on increasing individual social media presence using Facebook, Twitter, YouTube, and Instagram. Her branding, popular music and MySpace examples were a big hit with the audience! There were approximately 40 participants, and Liz did a great job answering ALL of their questions. Thanks Liz!

—BRETT BRYNGELSON, PROGRAM SPECIALIST
FOR *MUSICARES/GRAMMYS*

Liz helped Jukin Media with our initial launch party campaign, which included PR, social media and cause marketing for the Rob Drydek Foundation to reach our primarily 18-34 male demographic. This was a last minute campaign, and within 1 month, she helped us fine-tune our message, publish a press release, get key influencers to the launch party, and our social media fans increased on Facebook and Twitter by over 100%.

—JON SKOGMO, FOUNDER AND CEO OF *JUKIN MEDIA* INC.,
LOS ANGELES, CA

@LizHKelly @GoodyAwards strategically helped us from early on thru launch to develop a global marketing campaign including press releases, social media and photography for @ComedyGivesBack 24 Hours of Comedy benefiting Malaria No More that contributed to our 100 million impressions in 2 weeks resulting in winning the IAWTV Best Live Event Award. We were thrilled to leverage the Comedy Gives Back platform to honor Budd Friedman with the Golden Goody Award.

—@AMBERJLAWSON @COMEDYGIVESBACK, LOS ANGELES, CA

Liz's UCLA Extension New Media Marketing online class was tremendously useful to me professionally and personally, and I have already begun to deploy some of the learnings in my consulting practice.

—JIM E. SCHIEFELBEIN, CHICAGO, ILLINOIS

Thank you Goody PR and Liz H Kelly for helping us take our brand story to the next level for our Personalogy Game! We appreciate the powerful storytelling process that you took us through to rethink our positioning in a more playful way that emotionally connects with the media, customers and retailers. As a result, we now have Walmart interested in putting our games in their stores for Christmas! We can't thank you enough!

—MICHELLE BURKE, CREATIVE DIRECTOR AND
CO-FOUNDER, PERSONALOGY GAME

Book Endorsements

Follow the advice in this book. It will not only help you become better at the PR game, but become a better writer and better marketer, as well.

—Jess Todtfeld, CSP, former TV producer at *ABC*, *NBC*, and *FOX*, media trainer, speaker, and author (*Media Secrets*)

Kelly's booked thousands of media interviews for PR clients, including CNN, CBS Health Watch, FOX News, USA Today, The Wall Street Journal, NPR and more, making 8-Second PR a go-to guide for anyone with a brand story to promote.

—Bill Harrison, co-founder, *Radio–TV Interview Report* (RTIR) and *National Publicity Summit*

It was like Christmas morning waking up every day working with Liz Kelly on our PR. She partnered with us to develop new and innovative strategies for media stories, events and promotions! And now, you can find all of her secrets in this must-read book!

—Debbi DiMaggio, Realtor to the Stars, *Highland Partners* co-founder, philanthropist, and author of three books, including *The Art of Real Estate*.

I've worked with Liz for a number of years and the digital marketing strategies in 8-Second PR will help you not only engage influencers online, but it can help build Worth-of-Mouth Marketing to reach more people every day. And the photo and video storytelling tips are invaluable for social media marketing.

—Lindsay Mauch, Founder of LTM Digital (a Social Media
and Digital Marketing Agency), Social Media Instructor, and
Chapter President, *Social Media Club Los Angeles*

Working with Liz on the PR for her first book launch, she showed incredible insights on unique angles to pitch media outlets. And it's no surprise that she transitioned out of a corporate job into media and publicity because she intuitively understands the reporter's needs. This innovative how-to guide is a must read for anyone wanting to understand the method behind the madness of the PR world.

—Jamie Feldstein, former journalist and media relations
expert, and now licensed marriage and family therapist

About the Author

Author, speaker, Goody PR and *Goody Awards* CEO/Founder Liz H. Kelly is passionate about magnifying brands, experts and causes through marketing, PR, and social media campaigns with a powerful story that breaks through the noise. After working for *Fox Interactive Media/Myspace, Paramount Pictures, Sprint PCS*, and LA startups, Liz decided to use her marketing experience for GOOD full-time in 2008. As a published author with over 500 media hits (print, radio and TV interviews) over five years for one dating book (*Smart Man Hunting*), Kelly and her work have been featured on *CNN, FOX News, KCBS, KTLA, USA TODAY, The Chicago Tribune, Cosmopolitan, Buzzfeed, BBC Radio* and more.

Kelly also teaches digital marketing at *UCLA Extension, is a Social Media Club Los Angeles Board Member,* and is a digital influencer and speaker at industry conferences. Liz is a *Johns Hopkins University Carey School of Business* alumna, an Autism Advocate, and had a darkroom for processing photographs in her basement at age 17.

Websites

http://8SecondPR.com
http://GoodyPR.com
http://goodyawards.com
Follow @LizHKelly and @GoodyAwards on *Twitter, Facebook,* and *Instagram* (25k+ followers across social).

Made in the USA
Monee, IL
30 December 2022